INSTRUCTOR'S MANUAL

to Accompany

WRITING and READING ACROSS the CURRICULUM

Fourth Edition

LAURENCE BEHRENS
University of California, Santa Barbara

LEONARD J. ROSEN
Bentley College

HarperCollins*Publishers*

CONTENTS

Contents

Contents

A NOTE ON THE QUESTIONS

Students should be advised to read the *headnotes,* to master information about the author and the work that should be incorporated in some form into their syntheses and critiques.

There are two sets of *questions* in each chapter. One set (Review Questions, Discussion and Writing Suggestions) follows each reading selection. Another set (Synthesis Activities) follows the last set of Discussion and Writing Suggestions in each chapter.

The *Review Questions* are factual. Someone who has carefully read the preceding selection should be able to correctly answer these questions in a few sentences. The Review Questions are designed simply to facilitate recall and not to delve into the broader implications of the reading; they may be viewed as a helpful and necessary step in preparing a summary. The *Discussion and Writing Suggestions* are designed to stimulate further thought about the issues discussed in the reading selections; there are no "correct" answers, and answers are not necessarily confined within the boundaries of the reading selection itself. The Discussion and Writing Suggestions, therefore, should be helpful in preparing students to write syntheses or critiques. Or they may serve as alternate writing assignments to the Synthesis Activities. Either used exclusively or in combination with the synthesis activities, they allow the student to develop imaginative, personal, or simply less structured essays.

The *Synthesis Activities* following each unit are designed to give the student practice in the skills that are the focus of Part I.

SAMPLE SYLLABI FOR *WRITING AND READING ACROSS THE CURRICULUM,* FOURTH EDITION

In these sample syllabi we suggest two of the possible classroom approaches to the material in *Writing and Reading Across the Curriculum,* Fourth Edition. For each week, we offer reading and writing suggestions; instructors will want to modify these to suit the needs of their own classes. In both syllabi, the preliminary material from Part I (summary, critique, synthesis, introductions, conclusions, thesis statements, and quoting and citing sources) has been integrated into the subject units of the anthology (Part II) so that students may reinforce their writing and reading skills as they work on the anthology material. Teachers who wish to loosen some of the rigor of the synthesis approach (based on the questions at the end of each chapter) may want to assign the less academic Discussion and Writing Suggestions following the individual selections.

Syllabus 1

This syllabus assumes a ten-week course that meets three times per week. Students read the five chapters in Part I and complete reading and writing assignments for three chapters in Part II.

Week 1

A. Read "A Note to the Student."
Read Chapter 1, Summary and Paraphrase.

B. Read Newman, "American Nightmares" (Chapter 7, "Is America in Decline?")and write a summary. Small group exercise: students compare summaries in order to determine essential information.

C. Read Gandhi, "Still the Promised Land" and Krauthammer, "America in Decline? What Nation Are These People Looking at?" Write a summary of one article. Small group exercise: students compare summaries in order to determine essential information.

Week 2

A. Read Chapter 3, Synthesis.

B. Read Ashbrook, "A View from the East" and Branfman, "Economic Rebirth in a Post-Industrial World" (Chapter 7). Write a summary of one article. Submit for grade.

C. Read Kennedy, "Managing America's (Relative) Decline" and Percy's "July Fourth" (Chapter 7). Infer relationships among selections in Chapter 7, "Is America in Decline?"

Week 3

A. Read Chapter 4 on writing thesis statements. Draft three theses based on your reading in Chapter 7. Each thesis should be written at a different level of difficulty. Write three outline sketches of the papers that would follow from these working theses. Choose one outline and working thesis and begin rough draft of a paper.

B. Read Chapter 5 on quoting and citing sources. Scan the readings in the chapter and choose six or so quotations that you feel are pertinent to the draft you are writing.

C. Rough draft due.

Week 4

A. Read Chapter 2, Critique. Read Edwards, "Is the New Man a Wimp?" and Lester, "Being a Boy" (in Chapter 9, "Gender Identity"). For both, make notes towards writing of a critique (but don't actually write the critique).

B. Draft a critique of Edwards or Lester.

C. Read Masters, Johnson, and Kolodny, "Gender Roles" (Chapter 9).

Week 5

A. Revision of paper on "Is America in Decline?" due.

B. Read Jewett, "Tom's Husband" and Coman, "Who's Minding the Children?" (Chapter 9).

C. Read Merser, "Men, Women, Equality, and Love." Prepare a one-page proposal of a paper you would like to write, based on the readings in Chapter 9. Small group exercise: students critique one another's proposals.

Week 6

A. Conference in lieu of class.

B. Conference in lieu of class.

C. Draft of paper due.

Week 7

A. Read DeGeorge, "The Case of the Collapsed Mine" (in Chapter 11, "Business Ethics").

B. Read and write a summary (to be graded) of Cavanagh, "Ethics in Business" (Chapter 11).

C. Read "Peter Green's First Day" (Chapter 11).

Week 8

A. Read Bok, "Whistleblowing," and Vandivier, "Why Should My Conscience Bother Me?" (Chapter 11).

B. Read Carr, "Is Business Bluffing Ethical?" and Blodgett, "Showdown on 'Business Ethics'" (Chapter 11). Prepare notes for writing a critique of Carr. (Do not write a critique.)

C. Final draft of paper (on "Gender Identity") due.

Week 9

A. Read Boisjoly, "The Challenger Disaster," and Lewis, "Babbitt" (Chapter 11).

B. Prepare one-page proposal of paper you plan to write on the topic of "Business Ethics." Conference in lieu of class.

C. Conference in lieu of class.

Week 10

A. Rough draft of paper due. Group work — editing.

B. Group work — editing.

C. Semester review.

Final exam: Final draft of paper on "Business Ethics" due.

Syllabus 2

This syllabus provides for more reading and writing assignments than Syllabus 1. Naturally, the number of reading and writing assignments may be reduced to suit the needs of the particular class. In any case, we recommend no more than six or seven formal writing assignments during the course of a fifteen-week term. (Even if your students can handle more, you probably can't!) Other assignments may be informal, ungraded writing done in notebooks. These may include journal entries and other pre-writing activities, responses to the readings, or responses to Review and Discussion and Writing Suggestions following the readings. You may wish to schedule regular peer review sessions during which students evaluate each other's rough drafts.

Week 1

Reading Assignments
   A Note to the Student
   Chapter 1: "Summary and Paraphrase"

Writing Assignments
   Summary of Bird, "College is a Waste of Time and Money"
      (Chapter 2)
   or Bok, "Whistleblowing" (Chapter 12)

Week 2

Reading Assignments
   Chapter 6: "Obedience to Authority"
      Milgram, "Perils of Obedience"
      Reviews by Herrnstein, Baumrind, Meyer

Writing Assignments
   Summary of Milgram, "The Perils of Obedience"
   or Writing Suggestion following one of the readings

Week 3

Reading Assignments
   Chapter 3: "Synthesis" ("The Description Synthesis," pp 59-81)
   Chapter 4: "Thesis, Introductions, Conclusions"
   Chapter 6: "Obedience to Authority" (continued)
         Jackson, "The Lottery"

Writing Assignments
   Description Synthesis of Milgram, Herrnstein, Baumrind, Meyer
   (Describe the controversy over the Milgram experiment.)
   or Writing Suggestion following one of the readings

Week 4

Reading Assignments
   Chapter 6: "Obedience to Authority" (continued)
         Lessing, "Group Minds"
         Crockett, "My Buttoned-Down Students"
         Gibson and Haritos-Fatouros, "The Education of a
            Torturer"

Chapter 2: "Synthesis" ("The Argument Synthesis," pp. 81-114)
Chapter 5: "Quoting and Citing Sources"

Writing Assignments
Writing Suggestion following one of the readings or
Argument Synthesis or Comparison-Contrast Synthesis. (Compare and contrast some of the cases of obedience discussed in Obedience to Authority chapter, using criteria of your own choosing. Or select one of the Synthesis Activities at the end of the chapter.)

Week 5

Reading Assignments
Chapter 11: "Business Ethics"
DeGeorge, "The Case of the Collapsed Mine"
Cavanagh, "Ethics in Business"
selected "Cases for Analysis and Discussion"

Writing Assignments
Writing Suggestion following one of the selections
or Synthesis Activity at the end of the chapter.

Week 6

Reading Assignments
Chapter 10: "The Brave New World of Genetic Engineering"
Huxley, "Brave New World"
Chamberland, "Genetic Engineering: Promise and Threat"
Virshup, "Perfect People"
The New Republic "What Price Mighty Mouse?"

Writing Assignments
Synthesis Activity at the end of the chapter
or Writing Suggestion following one of the readings.

Week 7

Reading Assignments
Chapter 10: "The Brave New World of Genetic Engineering" (continued)
Hunt, "The Total Gene Screen"

Rifkin, "A Heretic's View of the New Bioethics"
Gould, "On the Origin of the Specious Critics"
Chapter 2: "Critical Reading and Critique"

Writing Assignments
Critique of an author in this chapter
or Writing Suggestion following one of the readings.

Week 8

Reading Assignments
Chapter 13: "AIDS: Public Good vs. Private Rights"
Abbott Labs, "AIDS: The New Epidemic"
"Proposition 102"
Restak, "When a Plague Looms, Society Must
  Discriminate"
Nelson, "Blaming the Victim"

Writing Assignments
Critique of any selection in unit
or Writing Suggestion following one of the readings
or Synthesis Activity at the end of the chapter.

Week 9

Reading Assignments
Chapter 13: "AIDS: Public Good vs. Private Rights" (continued)
Altman, "The Moral Crusade"
Buckley, "Identify All the Carriers

Writing Assignments
Critique of any selection in unit
or Writing Suggestion following one of the readings
or Synthesis Activity at the end of the chapter.

Week 10

Reading Assignments
Chapter 12: "AIDS: Public Good vs. Private Rights" (continued)
Tierney, "Straight Talk"
Sontag, "The Way We Live Now"

Writing Assignments
Writing Suggestion following one of the readings
or Synthesis Activity at the end of the chapter.

Week 11

Reading Assignments
Chapter 13: "Bartleby: Why Does He Prefer Not to?"
Melville, "Bartleby, the Scrivener"

Writing Assignments
Writing Suggestion following "Bartleby."

Week 12

Reading Assignments
Chapter 13: "Bartleby: Why Does He Prefer Not to?" (continued)
Beja, "Bartleby Is a Schizophrenic"

Writing Assignments
Critique of Beja *or* Writing Suggestion following one of the readings.

Week 13

Reading Assignments
Chapter 13: "Bartleby: Why Does He Prefer Not to?" (continued)
Franklin, "Bartleby Is Christ"
Barnett, "Bartleby Is Marx's Alienated Worker"

Writing Assignments
Critique of Franklin or Barnett *or* Writing Suggestion following one
of the readings.

Week 14

Reading Assignments
Chapter 13: "Bartleby: Why Does He Prefer Not to?" (continued)
Marx, "Bartleby Is Melville"
Barber, "Bartleby Is a Woman"

Writing Assignments
Critique of Marx or Barber *or* Writing Suggestion following one of the readings.

Week 15

Writing Assignments
Synthesis Activity at end of chapter.

OBEDIENCE TO AUTHORITY

6

As with the three earlier editions of *Writing and Reading Across the Curriculum,* this edition includes a chapter on obedience to authority, the central feature of which is the Milgram experiment. New to this edition are selections by novelist Doris Lessing, short-story writer Shirley Jackson, and psychologists Janice Gibson and Mika Haritos-Fatouros.

As in the other editions of WRAC, this chapter asks—how much obedience to figures of authority is necessary to ensure social well-being? When individuals refuse to relinquish any of their own autonomy for the welfare of the larger group, anarchy may result. When the state refuses individuals the right to exercise personal freedoms, totalitarianism follows. The balance civilized people try to strike between these extremes is the territory addressed in the selections here. The chapter begins with an essay by novelist Doris Lessing, who sets the issue of obedience in the context of Western civilization's greatly-prized individualism. Lessing values individual effort, but she believes us to be "group animals," a characterization that students might find offensive. Lessing cites examples to defend her claim, and she wonders why we do not accept and teach our children to be wary of the obedient streak in our natures. She refers to the experiments of Stanley Milgram, a psychologist who in the 1960s conducted experiments to determine the conditions under which people can be expected to obey immoral orders—orders that appear to result in the injury of persons for no justifiable reason. These experiments raised a furor, and we include three reactions of Milgram's work—one clearly favorable (Herrnstein), one unfavorable (Baumrind), and one somewhat ambiguous (Meyer). Milgram's account of his experiments, followed by these three reviews, can form a sub-unit on the ethics of experimenting on humans.

Three selections follow those devoted to the Milgram experiments, the first two of which lay the problems of obedience directly at the feet of students. Both Larry Crockett's "My Buttoned-Down Students" and Gibson and Haritos-Fatouros's "The Education of a Torturer" claim that students are hardly exempt from the tendency to obey. Crockett's piece can get students thinking about the extent to which they disobey in the classroom and the extent to which disobedience is the obligation of an engaged learner. Gibson and Haritos-Fatouros discuss the training of torturers in Greece—a subject safely removed from students. But then the authors draw a disturbing analogy to rituals of fraternity initiation. A second sub-unit in the chapter would focus on the obedience in the lives of students. The readings would include Lessing, Milgram, Crockett, and Gibson and Haritos-Fatouros. The chapter ends with Shirley Jackson's well-known story, "The Lottery." Many students will have read the story, but likely not in the context of the observations by Milgram and Lessing. Students may be able to recognize in Jackson's fiction our common and necessary need to obey, taken to hideous ends. Obliquely, disobedience is considered by characters in the story but then is quickly discounted. You might want to ask students how Jackson raises the issues discussed in Milgram and Lessing. As in other chapters, literature can serve as a counterpoint to other (more academic) ways of knowing.

Group Minds (p. 161)

DORIS LESSING

Lessing provides a good opportunity for students to challenge their own views about individuality. Though we may be "group animals," according to Lessing, when we (Westerners) look in the mirror we see rugged individualists staring back. Students may style themselves as individualists—and if they do, Lessing will raise questions for them. The selection provides a good entry into the discussion of obedience. Lessing anticipates the discussion of Milgram, without being totally absorbed in it—so the context is broader, and the likelihood is greater that students will be interested.

Review Questions

1. The flattering portrait: that we, as citizens of a free society, are free to express our opinions and to make individual choices.
2. We in the West are "helpless against all kinds of pressures . . . to conform in many kinds of ways" because we are group-oriented people who would rather betray our own view of the world than risk ostracism. Lessing claims that it is the "hardest thing in the world to maintain an individual dissident opinion" and remain a member of a group.
3. Lessing refers to a group of experiments designed to test the extent to which individuals can stand against group opinion or the opinion of an authority figure.
4. Lessing is advocating that we use the information gained in the "obedience experiments" to change our behavior for the better. Though most of us have bowed at one time or another to group pressure, we do not like to contemplate the darker implications of such behavior. The results of the obedience experiments are rarely made public so that people can learn from them. Lessing proposes that, beginning in elementary school, people

be made aware of their tendency to obey. This would be a first step to "setting people free from blind loyalties, obedience to slogans, rhetoric, leaders and group emotions."

The Perils of Obedience (p. 167)

STANLEY MILGRAM

Milgram's popularized account of his experiments appeared in *Harper's* in 1973. In this piece, Milgram summarizes his experimental findings in what some might term perversely dispassionate detail. Subjects are seen anguishing over the course of action they should take; their moral dilemmas can be quite painful for readers, some of whom will—like Diana Baumrind—question the ethics of an experiment that causes such emotional distress. On finishing the selection, students should be clear on Milgram's principal experimental design and its significant variations.

Review Questions

1. Obedience is a basic structure of social life. Systems of authority are required by all communal living. Where authority is established, commands must be respected or anarchy will ensue. Social order is premised on a given amount of obedience.
2. The dilemma inherent in the issue of obedience is an ethical one: Why should a person obey a command that conflicts with personal conscience?
3. A summary of the obedience experiments will be based on paragraphs 4 through 24. Writing a summary will be tricky in that students often have difficulty articulating the difference between the experimenter's confederate—the "learner," and the actual subject—the "teacher." We suggest that each student write a summary and then work in groups to agree on essential information. Various groups can then share their collective summaries—which, if accurate, will cover the same territory.
4. Experts predicted that virtually all subjects would refuse to continue shocking victims beyond 150 volts. Only 4 percent would continue to 300 volts, and only 0.1 percent would continue to the end of the shock board. As Milgram states, "These predictions were unequivocally wrong. Both college students at Yale and adults from the general population in New Haven were fully obedient roughly 60 percent of the time."
5. Milgram refutes these assumptions, based on an experimental design in which subjects could choose their own levels of shock (as opposed to being ordered to increase shocks incrementally). In this design, subjects overwhelmingly selected lower levels of shock, disproving (according to Milgram) the theory about innate aggressiveness. The second assumption,

that only a lunatic fringe would shock learners with the maximum voltage, is undermined by Milgram's finding that nearly two-thirds of all subjects administered the maximum shock. See paragraphs 82 through 86.

6. Arendt contended that the portrayal of Eichmann as a sadistic monster was incorrect—that he was, rather, an uninspired, middle-level bureaucrat simply doing his job. Milgram's conclusions, that nearly two-thirds of his subjects became agents in a destructive process, seem to corroborate Arendt's thesis.

7. See paragraph 97: The essence of obedience is "that a person comes to view himself as the instrument of carrying out another person's wishes, and he therefore no longer regards himself as responsible for his actions." All essential features of obedience follow once this shift has occurred: The "agent" feels responsibility to a figure of authority, not to the victim.

8. When subjects did not need to take direct responsibility for inflicting painful shocks, 36 of 40 proceeded in their roles—resulting in the learners being shocked at the maximum level.

9. It was a fragmentation of the total human act that led to the atrocities of the concentration camps in World War II. Eichmann shuffled papers and gave orders that he did not have to see carried out; thus he did not face the direct effects of his actions. Persons at the other end of the chain of command, those who actually gassed victims, could claim that they were merely following orders, thus relieving themselves of responsibility for their acts. With no one person responsible for the total act (i.e., designing and implementing the Final Solution), no one person was forced to live with the ramifications of that act. Every person in the chain had a convenient means of absolving him- or herself of guilt.

Review of Stanley Milgram's Experiments on Obedience (p. 184)

RICHARD HERRNSTEIN

Herrnstein discusses the various criticisms of the experiment, especially emphasizing the question of ethics. He argues his position well, and students may want to study how he accepts the reasonableness of opposing views, only to discount them later.

Review Questions

1. Individuals must relinquish some control in order for the community to function smoothly. "A degree of obedience is the given in human society." says Herrnstein.

2, 3. The "critical dilemma" is the balance between excessive and reasonable individualism. Americans value a society in which personal conscience is a vital determiner of behavior. But individualism carried to excess ends in anarchy.

4. The experiment received mixed reviews because it was so controversial. Some objected because they didn't want to acknowledge new and awful truths about human nature. Others, whom Herrnstein accuses of not wanting to admit their surprise at the experiment's findings, complained that social scientists never discover anything we don't already know. Still others objected to the level of deception practiced in the experiment.

5. Herrnstein believes that some deception is unavoidable in social scientific research. Short of placing subjects in hazardous conditions, which would be criminal, researchers can do little but manipulate ordinary experience (by deceiving subjects) in order to observe how human beings behave under stress.

Review of Stanley Milgram's Experiments on Obedience (p. 188)

DIANA BAUMRIND

Baumrind's criticism of Milgram's experiment contrasts sharply with Herrnstein's praise. Students should be able to distinguish the two lines of Baumrind's attack—the procedural and the ethical.

Review Questions

1. Subjects might volunteer for an experiment for public reasons: to have a stimulating experience, to acquire knowledge, to make a contribution to science. Subjects might volunteer for a private reason: to be in contact with someone who has psychological training. The subject's characteristic dependent attitude is due to private needs and the experimental condition, which requires following directions.

2. A laboratory is not a suitable setting for an experiment in obedience because subjects are inclined to be obedient in unfamiliar surroundings. The subject is also highly suggestible—a function of his volunteering. Baumrind claims that the baseline for obedience or suggestibility is probably higher in a lab than elsewhere.

3. Baumrind gives four reasons why the Milgram experiment was potentially harmful: (a) The experiment could affect the subject's self-image or ability to trust adult authorities in the future. (b) The subject's feeling of personal responsibility for acts committed might not be completely erased after the

experimenter explains the procedure. (c) The subject might feel as though he's made a fool of himself. (d) The subject might find it difficult to express anger at the hoax.
4. (a) When following orders, subordinates in Nazi Germany had no reason to believe that officers were kindly disposed to them or to their victims. (b) The subordinates followed orders in a social context in which it was acceptable to brutalize others. (c) In Germany, the victims were regarded as subhuman. None of these conditions applied to Milgram's experimental setting.

Review of Stanley Milgram's Experiments on Obedience (p. 195)

PHILIP MEYER

Meyer takes issue with Milgram's implied assertion that what the world needs is a more defiant citizenry. One value of having a civil order is to relieve people of agonizing over the many decisions they make daily. Another value is that chains of authority work. A society in which everyone stopped to weigh ethical dilemmas would not function. Meyer touches on a distinction raised by others in the chapter, between code ethics and situation ethics. Students would do well to learn this distinction and then to apply it in their discussions of obedience.

Review Questions

1. Powers said that as a soldier his job was to follow orders—that superiors were the ones who should concentrate on the larger implications of a military operation.
2. Code ethics: one's system of belief that attempts to resolve all dilemmas before one ever confronts them in fact. A rigid set of ethical rules cannot solve the obedience dilemma because compliance is a situational behavior. The decision to obey or disobey depends (for Meyer) on the nature of the authority requesting the obedience.

My Buttoned-Down Students (p. 199)

LARRY J. CROCKETT

Crockett's brief essay appeared in the "My Turn" column is the October 22, 1984 edition of *Newsweek*. Students will quickly recognize the challenge posed by Crockett, who finds his students to be buttoned-down conservatives who fail to challenge received wisdom. Crockett contrasts his students with the radicals of the 1960s and 70s, and one senses his lament. The essay should provoke response. Do students see themselves incapable of making a "spirited challenge" to received wisdom? Do they agree in principle with the value of such a challenge? Do they accept as a fact that the golden age of academics has passed? Do they see themselves at all remiss in their intellectual responsiblities? These and similar questions could well lead to heated exchanges.

Review Questions

1. Crockett's worries about students who do not challenge his interpretation of things. He would prefer to see students exhibit "a certain ragamuffin, barefoot irreverence."
2. "The subjects I teach [religious studies and philosophy] . . . subsist on well-formed questions and substantial debate."
3. Crockett considers genuine debate about opinions as the essential feature of legitimate academic study. There is no such debate that he can see now, so he recalls the 1960s, a time in which students challenged all received wisdom, as a golden age of academics.
4. At its worst, passion can be a dogmatic, undemocratic substitute for carefully reasoned thinking.
5. When students are secure about employment prospects, they have the luxury of radically questioning the status quo, since they needn't worry about earning money enough to live. Students who seek employment in more economically depressed times are less assured of their livelihoods and are less likely to attack the status quo, since they will have to depend on conditions as they are in order to support themselves and a family.

The Education of a Torturer (p. 202)

JANICE GIBSON
MIKA HARITOS-FATOUROS

Students know about the Holocaust—they know that millions of innocent people died in gas chambers. So widely publicized are these horrors that students may think they have no bearing on the ways people behave today. But as this article shows, obedience to malevolent authority is a problem in more recent times as well, not in only in Greece but potentially everywhere. The conditions that give rise to damaging obedience can be found across the globe—even on college campuses.

Review Questions

1. Sixteen Rorschach ink blot tests reports were submitted to fifteen experts for analysis to determine whether or not the experts could distinguish "normal" from "aberrant" traits. Half of the reports were taken from psychological profiles of Nazi officials while the other reports were taken from the profiles of both well-adjusted and severely disturbed Americans. The experts were unable to distinguish the reports of the Nazis from those of the Americans and judged an equal number of both to be well adjusted. The psychologists conclude that torturers are not "freaks"; they are "ordinary people."

2. There are three reasons for obeying or disobeying a figure of authority: First, the person whose family and school lives encouraged obedience will likely be responsive to an authority figure. Second and third—if "binding" experiences (those that made a person feel comfortable when he or she obeyed authority) are more prevalent and more compelling than experiences of "strain" (unpleasant associations with obedience), individuals are more likely to obey an authority figure. The authors expand Milgram's theories to explain how torture can occur over an extended period of time when *no* authority figure exists. The authors believe that "torture can be taught" through techniques that reduce strain and increase binding.

3. Five attributes were sought when recruiting potential torturers: First, hostile attitudes towards potential victims (because of differences in politics, religion, etc.); second, "the ability to keep your mouth shut"; third, the tendency to show aggression; fourth, intelligence and strength; fifth, being "their man"—demonstrating an ability to report on peers and to follow orders blindly.

4. The "Third Wave" was an experiment conducted by a high-school teacher to demonstrate the process by which people might have become Nazis in World War II. Conducted over five days, the experiment enlisted students through binding rituals such as membership cards, chants, slogans, etc.

5. The Stanford prison experiment was a six-day experiment similar in nature to the "Third Wave." College students were divided into two groups, guards and prisoners, and were told to act their respective roles. Though there was no specialized training, "guards" began to exhibit traits— aggression, the will to be powerful—similar to those exhibited by Greek military recruits.

The Lottery (p. 211)

SHIRLEY JACKSON

New to this edition, Shirley Jackson's famous story has both the advantage and disadvantage of being widely known. Students familiar with it will not be shocked, as they were on a first reading, by the violence—and much of the effect of the story will be lost the second time around. Just the same, as they contemplate another reading students can bear in mind Milgram's and Lessing's views on obedience to authority. Why do the people in this town follow through with the ritual year after year? What is the power of ritual in people's lives? What is the force of a community's pressure to conform? Students who have read the story may not have seen any of the reactions it generated on publication. For a sample of these, see the Discussion and Writing Questions.

IS AMERICA IN DECLINE?

7

Many commentators, economists, politicians, and industrialists have taken on the question: Is America in decline? We have tried to reflect the variety of responses in this chapter's selections. We begin with Robert Reich's "American Morality Tale." Though students will not have read this before, the story will nonetheless be familiar, for it is the American success story: modest but dedicated and principled man makes good on his talents, secures his fortune, and becomes a pillar of the community. Students may know the story through adults who overcame hardship and were successful; students may also be striving to achieve for themselves the story's conclusion, and so find themselves in college. In either event, Reich's tale provides a point of reference for the chapter—the idealized version of what America and Americans can be.

If the story of Reich's character, George, represents important themes in American life, then writers like Katherine Newman, Tom Ashbrook, Fred Branfman, and Paul Kennedy offer counter themes, a heavy dose of real life. These authors argue that America's story is more complicated than George's. Katherine Newman is an anthropologist who has studied the phenomenon of "downward mobility," the disquieting and re-occurring movement of schooled and well-paid professionals *down* the socio-economic ladder, through no fault of their own. Tom Ashbrook, a journalist returning from several years in Japan, finds his country in moral and physical disrepair. Fred Branfman uses government statistics to define the scope of problems besetting our country. Paul Kennedy takes a broad, historical look at the rise and fall of great nations and concludes that decline—at least relative decline—is inevitable and should not shock us.

The views of those pre-occupied with America's troubles are balanced by Natwar Gandhi and Charles Krauthammer. Gandhi, an immigrant, finds flaws in the pessimism about America's fortunes. Gandhi looks to America's social and political resources and concludes that America is still a great nation. Krauthammer looks abroad and, taking the measure of American influence, concludes that America is an unrivaled superpower. An altogether different perspective on decline is offered in an excerpt from Walker Percy's novel, *Love in the Ruins.* Percy's fiction is ironic, and he injects some humor (along with some philosphy) into the discussion.

Is America in decline? If so, is the decline relative or absolute? Should our young people be concerned? Are they? The readings here will provide students with plenty of resources with which to draw conclusions. The entire chapter is premised on students' keeping up, at least minimally, with current events. Books and newspaper and magazine articles continue to be written about American competitiveness (or lack thereof), and the chapter lends itself to a student's looking outside the text for resources. Synthesis assignments might be cast as limited research papers that draw on selections in this chapter and readings that students identify.

An American Morality Tale (p. 226)

ROBERT B. REICH

Before students read Reich's morality tale, have them write their own parable describing a successful life in America. Students can compare efforts and then read Reich's selection. Rich comparisons can be made that call attention to the assumptions students have about hard work's eventual payoffs. The readings that follow Reich will prove more of a counterpoint if it is the student's own idealized version of America being challenged.

Review Questions

1. The four themes that emerge from the morality tale are, essentially, the core traits to which Americans aspire—traits perceived both as great strengths and as qualities that set Americans apart from people of other nations. These traits are humility, generosity, honesty, and industry.
2. Four American parables are embodied in George's story: "the flight from older cultures"; the "rejection of central authority and aristocratic privilege"; "the lure of the unspoiled frontier"; and "the struggle for harmony and justice."
3. As the four cultural parables illustrate, the aspirations of Americans are more utopian than objective. As such, they are too "vast and vague" to be realistically achieved. The principle that underlies American idealism is that we are, in the absence of "common history," bound together by "common hope."

American Nightmares (p. 234)

KATHERINE S. NEWMAN

Newman's anthropological study is disturbing precisely because it describes a world in which people play by the rules of hard work and self-sacrifice—and still lose. The implication of this selection are enormous. As Newman shows, it is a myth that one's fortunes are tied exclusively to one's efforts, as the America success story suggests. If it is larger forces at work shaping the lives of individuals, then individual commitment and dedication may not—in the end—count for much. Why should individuals sacrifice at all? One way of engaging students in this selection is to ask if they believe David's fate could befall them—or their parents.

Review Questions

1. David felt isolated and abandoned by his friends with whom he no longer shared common experiences and with whom he could no longer afford to socialize. He felt guilty for having uprooted and disappointed his children, yet frustrated by their resentment since he had made career moves with their welfare in mind. His relationship with his wife became strained, and he became resentful of her accusatory attitude at his continued failure to work.
2. Downward mobility occurs when skilled and well-educated individuals who have attained occupational and financial success suddenly experience a sharp reversal in their fortunes. The phenomenon is an ongoing, rather than an unusual, occurrence that affects over 20% of the American population.
3. The poor tend to originate and to remain at the bottom of the social and economic hierarchy. The downwardly mobile, by contrast, possess the skills, educations, and career experience that once enabled them to achieve (at least) a middle-class life style.
4. American culture, which values success and firmly believes in the ability of the individual to control his own destiny, is embarrassed by and fears the downwardly mobile. The downwardly mobile are therefore ignored, a tendency reinforced by both research groups and the media, who don't feel the problem is worthy of notice. The public remains uninformed of the problem and believes that individuals who slide *down* the ladder of success are somehow flawed and deserving of their misfortune.

A View from the East (p. 247)

TOM ASHBROOK

Tom Ashbrook is a persuasive journalist, and he paints an unflattering, almost alarmist portrait of an American that has lost its competitive—and moral—edge. Students might ponder the extent to which Ashbook has "bought into" the idealist themes of Reich's morality tale. To be sure, Ashbrook feels we have slipped. *From what* is the issue students will want to address. How realistic a view of America did Ashbrook begin with?

Review Questions

1. Two qualities that make America attractive to Ashbrook: its regard for individuality and its diversity—traits that are not encouraged in Asia. In the East, Ashbrook found the value placed on conformity and harmony to be "smothering."
2. The American qualities of hard work, realism, and resolve once inspired awe in Asians, who now look on Americans with disdain. To Asians, Americans have grown lazy and greedy. Asians believe that we consume too much and lack direction.
3. Asian cultures value harmony and the good of the group—traits that are not compatible with huge salaries. Asians believe that huge salaries inspire greed and potentially distract executives from a company's mission.
4. Ashbrook can't understand America's inaction in the face of the many problems he sees confronting us. He feels that we've retreated into selfish escapism, rather than sought solutions that could reverse our decline.
5. American children are permitted to discover and decide their futures for themselves, thereby fostering a sense of individualism and self confidence. Asian children are burdened from the start with an extensive set of rules that emphasize the importance of duty and self-denial. As a result, Asians seem to lack the "verve" and sense of adventure that inspires their American counterparts.
6. Ashbrook feels Americans should fight to retain their racial diversity, their sense of equality, their respect for the individual, and their insistence on women's rights.
7. Americans escape into fantasy and "the movies" rather than confront the forces that threaten them. They barricade themselves behind "burglar alarmed" walls and private schools instead of reclaiming their society from crime and bureaucracy.
8. If the American virtues of "freedom, liberty, and openness" were combined with the Asian work ethic and resolve, the world would benefit socially, politically, and economically.

Still the Promised Land (p. 259)

NATWAR M. GANDHI

Robert Reich wrote that the aspirations of Americans were more utopian than objective. Natwar Gandhi would agree, and he believes the pessimism of American commentators is a function of their idealism. Compared to an ideal, the real world always suffers. As an immigrant, Gandhi does not take freedom or national achievement for granted. His appreciation for the country implicitly challenges native-born naysayers to re-examine the basis of their pessimism. Why should it take a relatively new arrival to America to appreciate its political system and economic prosperity?

Review Questions

1. Keenan and Wilson are pessimistic because the real America falls short of the country they grew up believing in. We are not living up to our ideals. Keenan and Wilson focus on how far the U.S. has to go, rather than on how far it has come.
2. Gandhi measures America's accomplishments with such yardsticks as race relations—and in these terms he does not see America in decline.
3. Given the current rates of immigration and current U.S. birth trends, the U.S. population will no longer be represented by a white majority in 50 years. White birth rates have declined relative to that of other racial groups. Asians have replaced Europeans as the most common U.S. immigrants.
4. As an immigrant from a country whose citizens do not enjoy privileges common in the U.S., Gandhi can appreciate the American dream—however unrealistic it may have become. Americans, who have always known these privileges, are more apt to complain.

America in Decline? What Nation Are These People Looking at? (p. 262)

CHARLES KRAUTHAMMER

Krauthammer can be difficult for students: his style involves densely packed sentences, intricately shifting thought patterns, and references to events and controversies with which he assumes his readers are familiar. In other words, he gives his readers credit for having a certain degree of intelligence and knowledge. He has no use for jargon, but he frequently does employ irony, which can be confusing for readers not expecting it. Still, this article should be clear enough in its overall purpose and execution. And in its conclusions it serves as a strong counterpoint to several of the other articles in this chapter, so it is especially well suited for use in student syntheses.

Review Questions

1. After the introduction, Krauthammer discusses America's (1) wealth, (2) prestige, and (3) influence and power. He picks up these schemes from the quotation by an "eminent commentator": "American wealth, influence, prestige, and power are all declining . . ."
2. The United States has suffered a loss of relative wealth since World War II, Krauthammer argues, only because its allies were destitute after the war. The fact that they have regained their prosperity does not mean that in

absolute terms American wealth has declined. In fact, "the average American is today twice as wealthy as he was during the alleged peak of 1950."

3. There is now only one superpower, according to Krauthammer, because if we define a superpower (as former Soviet foreign minister Gromyko did) as "a country that has a say in every corner of the globe, and without whose say nothing truly substantial can be achieved in any such corner," then the Soviet Union has lost any such "say." The "say" of the United States, on the other hand, is greater than ever.

4. Starting in 1989, the "East bloc" of Soviet satellites—including East Germany, Hungary, Poland, Bulgaria, Romania, and Czechoslovakia—began breaking away from the Soviet Union. The Baltic States of Latvia, Lithuania, and Estonia, a part of the Soviet Union, began moving toward independence. (Lithuania did, in fact, declare its independence in March 1990.) And the client state of Nicaragua was lost to the Soviet Union when free elections there resulted in the defeat of the Marxist Sandinista party, under Daniel Ortega.

Economic Rebirth in a Post-Industrial World (p. 266)

FRED BRANFMAN

The carefully researched information in Branfman's article will be useful to students. Packed with facts and figures, it provides needed, concrete details that will improve student presentations. Students may need to be reminded that they can draw information from the article without endorsing Branfman's proposals for reversing America's decline.

Review Questions

1. The industrial world, based on a resource-dependent, capital-intensive economy, is in transition to a post-industrial world that is technologically and globally oriented. The major trends driving the transformation will be the emergence of the third world powers and the dominance of computer, bioscience, and telecommunications technologies.

   While it possesses the requisite raw materials to become a leader in the post-industrial revolution, the U.S. still must address the challenges of modernizing its inefficient, outmoded industrial base. Since the U.S. has the most invested in these old technologies and since these technologies are helping to maintain our present, strong global position, it will be harder to convince Americans to alter their attitudes about modernization. "Suffering" from no such position of strength, smaller and more flexible economies, hungry to experience their first success, will adapt more readily to the new economic imperatives.

2. The U.S. stands to lose its leadership position in industry, finance, and exports. Already, our hesitation to modernize has resulted in unfavorable economic trends. Unemployment, interest rates, inflation, and fiscal deficits are on the rise—while productivity and capital growth are declining.

3. Unlike borrowing in World War II, when debt was used to fuel industrial growth, today's borrowing has been used for nonproductive goals such as personal consumption, maintenance of military and social programs, short-term corporate liquidity, and support for an inflated wage base.

4. Modernization must "replace short-term growth as the organizing principle of American politics" because short-term goals will not result in the permanent modernization needed to participate in the technology dominated post-industrial world. Modernization will require vast capital infusions to both educate the young and retrain displaced workers. Without capable individuals adept at new technological developments, the social, industrial, and economic goals sought by the U.S. will not be achieved.

5. America's infrastructure is currently in serious disrepair. Its existing public amenities are obsolete and over burdened. Its educational system has grown mediocre, no longer a match for other systems in the world. Even America's once-dominant industrial sectors are no longer competitive with foreign industry.

6. For the U.S. to secure its place in the post-industrial world, it must invest heavily in industry, education, and infrastructure. The country must also invest internationally. New manufacturing and information technologies will increase productivity in both the industrial and service sectors. Renewed emphasis on education will be needed to train a competent, competitive workforce. Huge sums will be needed to repair the damaged infrastructure and the environment, both of which are vital to supporting the economy. Finally, the U.S. will need to expand its political and economic horizons to include international concerns. Exhausted foreign resources must be replaced and untapped markets identified.

The (Relative) Decline of America (p. 277)

PAUL KENNEDY

Kennedy's broad historical perspective may have a ring of invincibility about it to students, who may be intimidated by a scholar's poring through events of 400 years and arriving at this impressive synthesis. Still, students should be encouraged to challenge Kennedy's synthesis as an interpretation. Charles

Krauthammer does (indirectly), and students should look in that direction for help if they feel intimidated. In a curious way, Kennedy's argument shares an underlying feature of Katherine Newman's. Both writers argue that factors larger than the individual (for Newman, economic; for Kennedy, historical) are at work shaping an individual's fate at any given moment; to the extent this is so, the morality tale as told by Reich—the story celebrating individual effort—is seriously flawed.

Review Questions

1. The United States has enjoyed a disproportionately large share of the world's wealth (40%) while our size relative to other nations suggests that our share should be much smaller (16–18%). Thus, recent declines to our "proper" share means that Americans will now have an equitable wealth, relative to the rest of the world.
2. When unusual political, economic, and social forces converge in favor of a country, as was the case with the United States after World War II, that country may acquire more than its share of the world's wealth. When the circumstances change, it is only natural that the country's share will change. History validates this cycle, as can be illustrated by the ascent and subsequent decline of Spain, the Netherlands, and Great Britain.
3. Unlike Spain and the Netherlands, the United States is too large to sink into obscurity. Its geographical size, dense population, and abundant natural resources (compared to those of other countries) will enable the United States to sustain a significant presence in the world.
4. As history has demonstrated, the same political and economic forces that can result in a nation's rise to power can, if managed improperly, also result in decline. Just as the United States adapted and turned the postwar situation to its own gain, its failure to adapt to a new world order could lead to decline.
5. The challenges are as follows: First, special interests and the disruptions caused by frequent elections threaten to paralyze foreign policy and prevent clear, consistent policy making. Second, the U.S. "escapist urges" will hinder our relations with other countries, where predominant cultures and ideologies are quite different. Third, our government's system of checks and balances inhibits the flexibility and swift decision making needed to resolve international crises.
6. As long as there was a frontier, a physical space into which one could escape, Americans could avoid confrontation by simply moving west—a tendency that helped populate and develop the country. Today, the physical frontier is gone, and we simply cannot walk away from confrontations—local, national, or international.

July Fourth (p. 281)

WALKER PERCY

Percy is a challenging writer. His fiction is filled with allusions, and he is decidedly philosophical and ironic. But the challenge of reading Percy is well worth the effort, as students catch on to his sense of humor and his wry, running commentary on American life. The mood that Percy evokes in his novel *Love in the Ruins* is one of disrepair—both physical and moral. In both respects, the novel is related to other readings in the chapter: Fred Branfman writes of damage to America's infrastructure; Tom Ashbrook writes of a laxity of values. Neither of these writers retains much of a sense of humor about our predicament—but Percy certainly does. He also adds a philosophical dimension to the chapter by suggesting our predicament is not just a national matter but is also a personal, existential one. In *Love in the Ruins,* as in so much of literature, the state of the outer world (in this case, a world of disrepair) reflects the state of the inner. Percy confronts students with a very different perspective on America's position.

FAIRY TALES: A CLOSER LOOK AT "CINDERELLA"

8

Many feel that fairy tale literature should be off limits to aggressive, critical inquiry. "A Closer Look at 'Cinderella' " presents students with the opportunity to challenge this view. The readings here raise several questions: to what extent does critical inquiry illuminate? obscure? make something of nothing? In attempting to answer these questions, students will themselves invoke critical distinctions—perhaps similar to those we've included here: "Cinderella" may be approached as literature (Thompson and Yolen), as an occasion for psychological inquiry (Bettelheim), and as an example of gender-role typing (Kolbenschlag). By first reading the seven variants of "Cinderella," students will be able to make their own critical observations of the tale and then compare these with the observations made by professionals.

The current chapter represents a shorter version of that appearing in the third edition of *Writing and Reading Across the Curriculum*. We've included one selection by Bruno Bettelheim (not two), and have cut the selections by Zipes and Luthi. Otherwise, the chapter remains the same: We begin with a general introduction to fairy tale literature by Stith Thompson. Seven variants of "Cinderella" follow—the modern variants (which can be read as a subunit) being Disney, Sexton, and Gardner. The chapter ends with appraisals of the story by Bettelheim, Kolbenschlag, and Yolen.

The selections by Bettelheim, Kolbenschlag, and Yolen are each complex enough to make summaries worthwhile. The variants of the story lend themselves quite naturally to comparison and contrast. Opportunities for critique and argument abound, as students respond to the three critiques of "Cinderella."

Universality of the Folktale (p. 302)

STITH THOMPSON

This selection introduces Thompson's book, *The Folktale*. Thompson is a much-acclaimed folklorist and author of a six-volume *Motif-Index of Folk Literature* (1932–37, 1955–58, 2nd ed.). He concentrates here on the definition and history of the folktale, so the piece serves as an excellent overview to the chapter. We recommend that students read it directly before or after the variants of "Cinderella," and certainly before any of the critical examinations (namely, Bettelheim on "Oedipal Conflicts," Kolbenschlag, and Yolen). The final paragraph, and especially the final sentence, of Thompson's selection may be of special interest in establishing a mood of acceptance, or at least tolerance, of the various analyses of "Cinderella."

Review Questions

1. The storyteller is treasured by societies for providing information and amusement; inspiration (both secular and religious); and stimulation, as well as escape from routine.
2. Thompson claims that the most significant difference between the folktale and modern fiction is the traditional nature of folk material—tales that are not original in our sense of the word but that are passed along skillfully, bearing the authority of great age and constituting an act of conservation and reverence. Moreover, a folktale is meant to be listened to, not read. See paragraph 9.
3. Religion involves an attempt to understand personal, tribal, and cosmic origins; folktales are concerned generally with the "olden days." Their own origins are prehistoric, as are religion's.
4. The same tale is often dispersed widely throughout different parts of the world.

Seven Variants of "Cinderella" (p. 306)

We have placed the Perrault and Grimm versions of "Cinderella" first (*not* in chronological order), since these will be the most familiar to students. Four variants of the tale—Perrault, Grimm, Basile, and Tuan Ch'êng-shih—can be compared and contrasted as the so-called "traditional" renderings of "Cinderella." The three explicitly literary versions, by Disney, Sexton, and Gardner, might be compared as modern renderings. Comparisons and contrasts can obviously be drawn between the traditional and modern versions, with students arguing their preferences. This chapter presents students with an excellent opportunity to practice their own analysis of primary material before reading the analyses of professional commentators.

"Cinderella": A Story of Sibling Rivalry and Oedipal Conflicts (p. 340)

BRUNO BETTELHEIM

Bettelheim's analysis of "Cinderella," excerpted from *The Uses of Enchantment,* is one of the longer and more complex selections in the text. The author's psychoanalytic premise is summarized in Discussion Question 2, and students may profit by reading this question as they prepare for summaries or class discussions. The principal assumption—that complex unconscious and subconscious mechanisms explain human behavior—may be unacceptable to some students, especially as it is applied to the apparently innocent "Cinderella." Bettelheim's intricate analysis can demonstrate how arguments follow from their premises and how, if students want to object, they should examine premises and the consistency of their application.

Review Questions

1. Living among the ashes symbolizes sibling rivalry and Cinderella's debased condition.
2. The stepsisters in "Cinderella" may be a device "to explain and make acceptable an animosity which one wishes would not exist among true siblings."
3. A child experiencing sibling rivalry may feel that a parent is overlooking his or her welfare for the welfare of another child; the child may also feel persecuted at the hands of a sibling and believe that the parent is indifferent to this persecution.
4. Through Cinderella's triumph, the child gains "exaggerated hopes for his future which he needs to counteract the extreme misery" of sibling rivalry.
5. The fantasy solution to "Cinderella" is appropriate for children in that children do not believe they can actually reverse their fortunes; children also gain relief through fantasies of glory and domination over their siblings.
6. The child who identifies with Cinderella reasons that since Cinderella's goodness is eventually acknowledged by all—so too, one day, will his or her goodness be acknowledged.
7. By comparison with the vileness of the stepmother and stepsisters, the child feels his inadequacies and wrongdoings are minor. The vileness of these characters also justifies whatever harm is done to them in the story.

8. Cinderella's paradox is that she believes herself to be superior to her stepmother and stepsisters but at the same time feels that she deserves her degraded state.

9. In one story the father is the antagonist while in the other the stepmother and stepsisters are antagonists. Yet the antagonisms of each story arise out of Oedipal conflict.

A Feminist's View of "Cinderella" (p. 349)

MADONNA KOLBENSCHLAG

This feminist critique of "Cinderella" should stir discussion. Kolbenschlag is interested in the sociological effects of fairy tales and the ways in which they transmit cultural values. Those who accept a subservient role for women will doubtless disagree with the analysis—perhaps on the grounds that, yes, fairy tales do transmit cultural values and, in this case, correct ones; perhaps on the grounds that all intricate analyses of fairy tales lack validity (i.e., the argument that fairy tales are entertainment, nothing more).

Review Questions

1. Kolbenschlag believes that "Cinderella" has been successful in capitalist countries because the rags-to-riches content of the story has a Horatio Alger quality, communicating the idea that good fortune is won by merit (which is the essence of the Protestant work ethic).

2. Cinderella evokes intense identification because she represents the emerging self of a child enmeshed in a family network.

3. Cinderella's paradox is that she has accepted the internalized consciousness of the victim, while at the same time she believes herself ultimately worthy as a heroine. The paradox appeals because it counsels passivity.

4. Cinderella's association with ashes suggests degradation, affinities with virtues of the hearth, a vestal (serving) quality, and a period of grieving (with a transition to a new self).

5. The meaningless jobs that the stepmother gives Cinderella suggest that work at the hearth is not itself worthwhile and is to be endured only because it shows the heroine's virtues.

6. The slipper is at once seductive and destructive in that (a) the prince is enamored of the woman whose foot can fit into the tiny slipper, and (b) Cinderella's stepsisters must mutilate their feet in order to wear the slipper.

America's "Cinderella" (p. 355)

JANE YOLEN

In this article, Yolen distances herself from the views of feminists such as Kolbenschlag, and students should be able to say how. The author's condemnation of Disney's *Cinderella* may throw down a challenge to students who are fond of this variant. One hopes a discussion will ensue in which students reread the six variants and argue for or against Yolen's analysis.

Review Questions

1. Yolen contends that "Cinderella" is a story not of rags to riches, but of riches recovered and a stripping away of disguises. Cinderella is rich in spirit, deserving of praise all along.
2. Yolen believes that the feminist attack on "Cinderella" should be aimed at the American, candied versions of the tale. Older European and Oriental versions, she feels, feature a more resilient, resourceful heroine.
3. In Walt Disney's version of "Cinderella," the heroine is denied her "birthright of shrewdness, inventiveness, and grace under pressure."
4. We each have been Cinderella in that as children we have felt mistreated and forsaken. We have realized that action and intelligent decisions were needed to solve difficult problems.

GENDER IDENTITY: THE CHANGING RULES OF DATING AND MARRIAGE IN AMERICAN LIFE

9

The present chapter on Gender Identity is much changed from its earlier incarnations in the first and third editions of *Writing and Reading Across the Curriculum*. This chapter has fewer selections—six, and would be a good candidate for reading early in the semester. In addition, only one selection (by Margaret Edwards) remains from the third edition. We have tried to focus the discussion narrowly on dating and marriage. Students have knowledge of both: they date and are well aware of gender expectations of young adults; they also have observed parents interact. On both counts (indeed, some students may be married), they have the experience to respond to the material in this chapter.

At the age of 18, first-year college students are making the transition from late adolescence to young adulthood, a transition fraught with questions of gender: Now that they are preparing to enter the working world of adults, how will students identify themselves as adult men and women? How will gender roles explored in dating relationships carry over into marriage? How readily will students acknowledge that their images of masculine and feminine are culturally determined?

Masters and Johnson (with Kolodny) open the chapter with an overview of gender-role socialization, birth through adulthood. Students might be tempted to think of Masters and Johnson as the one "objective" view on gender identity. The tone may be social scientific and therefore may sound impartial and authoritative. Yet social science has its own assumptions, of course, and the chapter provides occasions for playing the "truths" of science off against the truths of fiction and reflection-by-essay. You may want to ask students, for instance, what they learn from Masters and Johnson, as compared to what they learn from Julius Lester, Margaret Edwards, Cheryl Merser, or Sarah Orne Jewett. Lester's, Edwards', and Merser's reflections and Jewett's short story make many of the same points arrived at by the social scientists. Are the observations of one more privileged than those of another?

Implicitly, the chapter asks students to do something quite difficult: to step back from the routine of everyday life and to observe what it means to be a young man or woman. What do students expect of a date or of a partner in marriage? How do students unconsciously operate according to one or another view of gender-role socialization? The questions force self-examination.

The chapter is meant to engage students, but in order for them to become engaged they must be willing to debate themselves, the authors of these selections, and their fellow students. In the classroom, discussions on gender often degenerate into a series of unexamined assertions about the way men and women are or should be. The chapter offers an opportunity to test these assertions, to push students into examining the beliefs that underlie traditional views of gender-role typing.

Gender Roles (p. 369)

WILLIAM H. MASTERS,
VIRGINIA E. JOHNSON,
ROBERT C. KOLODNY

The selection that opens this chapter reviews patterns of gender-role sterotyping from birth through adulthood. As would be expected from sex researchers Masters, Johnson, and Kolodny, the tone and method of this selection is social-scientific. The authors carefully cite research whenever they make broad claims. You might want to ask students to compare the tone of this piece with that of any other in the chapter (especially Julius Lester's recollection of his adolescence or Sarah Orne Jewett's story of role reversal in marriage).

Review Questions

1. Traditionally, American men are seen as "strong, courageous, self-reliant, competitive, objective, and aggressive." Women are seen as "intuitive, gentle, dependent, emotional, sensitive, talkative, and loving."

2. Earlier assumptions underlying psychological testing of gender role characteristics tended to view masculine and feminine traits on a single scale: one was judged either more or less masculine or feminine. A male who tested out of the masculine range or female out of the feminine were seen as "less emotionally adapted" than others. More recent tests assume that the classically gender specific traits (see Review Question 1) coexist within the same individual, who may exhibit masculine attributes such as aggressiveness in one sphere of activity but feminine ones (e.g., tenderness) in another.

3. The student will need to write a summary of the authors' sections on patterns of gender-role socialization at birth and infancy, in early childhood, in the school-age years, in adolescence, and in adulthood. The point of the summary should be that patterns of gender-role socialization are laid down at the earliest stages of development. Through toys,

television, dress, behavior of parents, choice of appropriate sports, and more, gender-appropriate behavior is clearly communicated in our culture.

4. The authors cite a variety of evidence to suggest that women are discriminated against: intellectually, with expectations that attractive women cannot be bright as well; financially, with women being paid less than men for comparable work; professionally, with women having greater difficulty than men reaching senior executive positions; and sexually, with women being touched, spoken to, or joked about in offensive ways. The authors do feel that times are changing; they cite examples of women entering traditionally male jobs and seeking or having achieved high public office or high-status occupations.

Being a Boy (p. 386)

JULIUS LESTER

Lester's essay is a short, accessible, funny—and bawdy—reminiscence of being an adolescent male. You might use the essay to discuss matters of style and tone (Lester is quite funny); to ask students to reflect on the gender issues of their own adolescence; and to discuss an issue common to other selections in the chapter: Socially defined gender roles limit and confuse us. We would more naturally (and healthfully) combine "masculine" and "feminine" traits if there were no social stigma for doing so. Note that Lester makes mention of his penis and masturbation. The context is hilarious, but some students may nonetheless be offended. Before students read the piece, an announcement concerning Lester's potentially offensive language might be in order.

Review Questions

1. As a boy, Lester judged his masculinity by externally defined standards. Could he play ball, win a fight, lie, climb trees? That he failed in these tests of boyhood plagued him as a youngster. We see Lester's essay informed with another point of view: he's since understood that being manly is an internal state and that no external tests need be applied to confirm masculinity.
2. As a boy, Lester thought girls "didn't have to do anything except be girls." By this he meant that, as far as he could tell, girls got to observe, sit, read, or play with dolls—passive or more meditative pursuits as compared with traditionally male activities.
3. The experience of dating put Lester in the position of being judged. Given that he was insecure about being a boy and young man, the prospect of judgment by a girl frightened him.

4. A summary of the essay should mention Lester's humor and the larger point he's making about gender identity. (See especially the final paragraphs.) An example: In a humorous essay, Julius Lester examines the rigid, often burdensome social codes for growing up male or female.

Is the New Man a Wimp? (p. 390)

MARGARET EDWARDS

Margaret Edwards startles readers with a question that might be on the minds of many but, in a liberated age would rarely be asked out loud. When the new man relinquishes his macho image, what will replace it, and will he be attractive both to himself and to women? The answer is not clear. Edwards casts doubt on the view that the evolution of men away from traditional gender identity is necessarily a happy development. Or, put another way, she suggests that the evolution is happy in one respect (men are more expressive of their feelings) but unhappy in another (overly sensitive men become self-absorbed and incapable of lasting commitment). From a feminist's own mouth springs a critique of the new man worthy of an arch-traditionalist. What Edwards offers is a view of gender identity in transition. If men and women are changing, what new identities are they taking on? Answers are far from clear—a state of affairs that might help students feel that their contributions to the discussion can be of value.

Review Questions

1. The point of Edward's anecdote is to establish a basis for remarking that many men today do not take initiative in dating and aren't interested in committing to relationships.
2. Edwards responds to this statement with sarcasm and bewilderment, remarking that the same has been said of dogs. The implication here is that men are looking for companionship without emotional involvement.
3. Ehrenreich describes the new man as more sensitive than his traditional counterpart but also more self-absorbed and less likely to want a lasting relationship with a woman. Ehrenreich would like to see both men and women cultivate traditional masculine and feminine traits that would promote a willingness to commit to relationships.
4. In response to the feminist revolution, many men have relinquished their assertive role to women. The men aren't ambitious at work, don't manage the money, and don't make suggestions regarding social activities. In sum, they are willing to follow the woman's lead. A reversal of roles has occurred, with many men evidently pleased with their lack of

responsibility and with many feminists fuming that the new men are wimps. The problem: ideal manhood, à la John Wayne, has been debunked but has not yet been replaced by an attractive alternative.

5. Traditionally, the woman stayed at home and offered "invisible support" to the man—that is, she allowed his worries, excitations, and ambitions to determine the relationship. The woman was present to nurture and to provide confidence. Now that the "new man" is taking on this traditionally female role, many (Laake, anyway) cannot stomach it. Edwards's point is that it is not enough to reverse roles. New gender identities need to be worked out.

6. A "wormboy" is a term that writer Deborah Laake uses to describe what she argues is a new and prevalent variety of young man. The wormboy is reluctant to marry and have children, and is indecisive, unambitious, and willing to let female companions "keep" him.

7. Edwards asserts that the sexes are not really polarized but are similar, even androgynous. For example, both her male and female acquaintances are torn between safe routines and new adventures, between boring jobs that pay and personal interests that don't, between the trust and safety of marriage and the excitement and perils of affairs, between having and not having children. Both worry about finding the right partner.

Men, Women, Equality, and Love (p. 397)

CHERYL MERSER

Merser's essay is a good candidate for critque. Students reading the selection can be advised to keep two sets of notes: one of the life-cycle (gender) patterns of the generation preceding Merser, and one on the patterning in Merser's generation. A line of response to Merser (b. 1951): the pattern she observes among her contemporaries does not fit the lives of today's students. (Most first-year college students in the 1990s will have been born after 1970.) In a critique, students could discuss what they take to be the life-cycle (gender) formula of their contemporaries.

Review Questions

1. Merser notes a decreased emphasis on adhering to the confining gender stereotypes that suffocated many marriages in the past. Still, she observes that "tension between the sexes" has never been greater. Couples don't communicate, the promised division of household responsibility has yet to be achieved, and infidelity plagues an astonishing number of relationships.

2. In the previous generation, the lives of men and women followed "parallel but complementary tracks" that "intersected at midlife," then separated and ran parallel again. At maturity, men and women led opposite but complementary lives. The man competed in the business world and provided for his family. The woman remained at home, raising the children and serving as emotional support for her husband. She had no distinct identity apart from her husband's and derived her worth vicariously through his successes. At midlife, the man, having proved himself in business and having grown aware of his mortality, discovered his more feminine, nurturing characteristics. The woman, meanwhile, having devoted her life to the service of others, now became restless to discover her own identity by exploring the world outside her home. Accordingly, she became more masculine, or assertive.

3. The life cycle that Erikson and others posited was a social phenomenon, not a biological one; still, men and women played their parts in the cycle as if they had no choice in the matter—as if a man's taking the traditionally masculine role and a woman's taking the traditionally feminine one was a fact of nature (that is, a "biological imperative"). Because role play is social in origin, not biological, it can change over time. In this article, Merser points out these changes, which she's observed in her own generation.

Who's Minding the Children? (p. 407)

CAROLYN COMAN

Carolyn Coman's interview of the three men in this selection was published in *Parenting* Magazine. Again, questions of authority come into play. In what ways is a piece appearing in a non-academic magazine as useful to students, as authoritative, as a chapter in a college-level text (i.e., Masters and Johnson)? The issue here is not better or worse, but the *ways* in which students read. How do they read textbooks differently than they do magazine articles? Urge students to articulate the differences. Aside from questions of authority, the three accounts in this selection directly call into question traditional gender-role stereotyping. How many men in the class would be willing to stay at home with kids? How many women would be content to be primary wage earners? The questions are not hypothetical, for in this selection couples decided to exchange traditional roles. See also Sarah Orne Jewett's story, "Tom's Husband," in which such an exchange of roles takes place.

Tom's Husband (p. 412)

SARAH ORNE JEWETT

Jewett's short story offers students an opportunity to discover how truths arrived at in fiction can be as powerful and authoritative as those arrived at by social science. Social science steps back from life to observe and report. A fiction writer immerses readers *in* life so that readers themselves observe and reflect. As a story, "Tom's Husband" may frustrate students, who might wish the ending had been otherwise. If this is the case with students in your class, ask that they write about the source of their frustration. Why should the male's assertion of a (then) husbandly prerogative be so unsettling today? Jewett's story also provides a fictional rendering of the accounts by the three house-husbands in "Who's Minding the Children?" You might ask students to compare tensions between husband and wife in the story with those of the real-life house husbands and their wives. Finally, Jewett's story has something to teach about the durability of the debate concerning gender-role socialization. The questions students debate in the 1990s have been debated in the 1890s. In this sense, "Tom's Husband" lends the chapter a historical, as well as literary, perspective.

THE BRAVE NEW WORLD OF GENETIC ENGINEERING

10

At first glance this science-based unit may appear somewhat daunting to nonscience oriented students. But the chapter is focused less on the scientific aspects of genetic engineering (though we do make some attempt to explain the process in the introduction and in the second selection) than on the social and moral dimensions of this new technology. As such, the premise underlying the chapter is a familiar one in our modern age. Our scientific and technological achievements have outstripped our social and moral development. This has been particularly true of weapons development, even prior to the nuclear age—and certainly since Hiroshima. But it is true of other areas, as well. Modern computers make it possible for us to store and retrieve vast quantities of information on everything and everybody. This is just the kind of technology that a police state would find essential. In another area, consider the moral (and legal) dilemmas that have been created by dramatic advances in medical technology. It is now possible to keep some dying patients alive almost indefinitely, as long as they are hooked up to a battery of medical equipment. Does this mean that they *should* be kept alive? The century's two most famous dystopias, *1984,* and *Brave New World,* are premised on technological developments: the former on ubiquitous television screens that can transmit as well as receive, making possible total surveillance of the citizenry; the latter on genetic developments that make possible birth without motherhood, and thus, the abolition of the family.

This unit considers some of the dilemmas created by the new science of genetic engineering. We begin with Huxley's *Brave New World* because this novel has come to represent a peculiarly modern nightmare of what happens when we abuse biological technology (indeed, from Shakespeare's time on, the title itself has come to indicate an ironic denial of the benefits of modernity). We chose Dennis Chamberland's "Genetic Engineering: Promise and Threat" to follow because it offers a clear survey of the history and the main issues involved in the controversy over genetic engineering. The remainder of the articles in the chapter explore various aspects of the genetic engineering debate. Amy Virshup considers the dilemmas that arise now that prospective parents can discover genetic defects of one kind or another in their unborn child. Morton Hunt considers the problems of genetic screening in the workplace. The next two articles were selected to be read against one another: Jeremy Rifkin, the chief critic of genetic engineering experiments argues against this new technology; biologist Steven Jay Gould responds to Rifkin's arguments. The commercial applications of genetic engineering—and in particular, the patenting of newly engineering animals—is considered next in an editorial from *The New Republic*. The chapter closes on a humorous note, with physician Lewis Thomas wondering about the possibilities of cloning our most able diplomats to solve future world problems.

One especially disturbing aspect of genetic engineering—the possibility of devising new types of biological weapons—is presented in Chapter One (on Summary and Paraphrase): David Suzuki and Peter Knudtson's "Biological Weapons: The Dark Side of Genetics." You may wish to remind your students of this article earlier in the text if you assign papers on the subject of genetic engineering.

Brave New World (p. 428)

ALDOUS HUXLEY

As we've suggested, the very phrase "brave new world" has become a part of the modern vocabulary, connotating an ironic attitude toward the value of supposedly modern improvements over more traditional ways of life. But how valid is Huxley's nightmare vision of the future? On a literal level, there seems little danger of the kind of world Huxley envisions coming to pass in the near future. No one (at least in our own country) is suggesting the mass production of human beings outside of the womb, nor the physical manipulation of human embryos to conform to the requirements of a rigid intellectual caste system. On a less literal level, there is considerably more room for debate as to whether or not we are now living (or are soon about to live) in a brave new world. You might ask your students how society encourages, perhaps even demands, an intellectual caste system. To what extent does society value uniformity, predictability, stability? What other values are sacrificed in the process? You may also wish to tell them something about the rest of the novel, particularly its emphasis on a hedonistic society. To what extent is our own society based on instant gratification? On sexual promiscuity? (Of course, Huxley wrote long before AIDS.) On the need for narcotics to evade unpleasant realities? On the contempt for all things "primitive" and ritualistic?

Review Questions

1. The Bokanovsky process, by splitting fertilized human ova into up to 96 identical eggs (resulting eventually in identical people) encourages social stability, because it suppresses individuality.
2. After boasting of the great number of adult individuals the London Center

had derived from a single egg, Foster remarks somewhat ruefully that "the tropical Centres" had "unfair advantages." "You should see the way a negro ovary responds to a pituitary!" he remarks, "It's quite astonishing when you're used to working with European material." Foster thus perpetuates the racial stereotype that in some respects blacks are physically superior to whites, though, of course, whites do all of the thinking and managing.

3. Alphas, Betas, Deltas, Gammas, and Epsilons, labels for the major castes in the brave new world, are born (or "decanted"), respectively, in increasing numbers, but also, respectively, with declining levels of intelligence. The controllers of brave new world have determined that there must be a limited number of highly intelligent people (Alphas, the administrators and managers) to run society, a somewhat greater number of somewhat less intelligent people (Betas, who are generally technicians), and so on, through relatively large numbers of workers (Deltas and below). Such an organized society assures a high level of social stability and a low level of dissatisfaction, since it is assumed that less intelligent people are more likely to be contented with their relatively menial jobs.

4. Scientists at brave new world had still not solved the problem of making humans mature as fast as animals, such as dogs or horses, so that they could do productive work at, say, six years old.

Genetic Engineering: How It's Done (p. 440)

RICHARD V. KOWLES

This will be a difficult piece for most students; it was difficult for *us,* since neither of us showed much aptitude for science during our school days. Still, even humanities types should be able to figure out the basic ideas that Kowles is dealing with (some of our scientifically inclined students may be able to help out here); and figuring out the basic ideas will serve the purpose here. Students don't have to be able to duplicate the gene-splicing process, based on Kowles's explanations, nor is it crucial for them to be able to accurately summarize what he says (though they might certainly *attempt* such a summary). They *should*—with the aid of the diagrams—develop some basic understanding of *how* gene splicing works.

Review Questions

1. As Knowles explains in paragraph 3, the four main steps of the DNA transfer process are (1) isolation or synthesis of the gene or DNA segment to be transferred; (2) cloning of the DNA segment; (3) transfer of the DNA

segment to the host cell or organism; (4) stabilization of the DNA segment in its new surroundings.

2. The chief methods of gene transfer: (1) incubation of host cells with purified DNA segments to be transferred; (2) injection of purified DNA into nuclei of host cells; (3) injection of whole chromosomes or transfer of chromosomes by cell fusion techniques; (4) using vectors to carry DNA segments into host cells.

3. Recombinant DNA allows for specific selection of genes to be transferred and specific sites to which they will be transferred in the host DNA, and it enables scientists to predict how the engineered organisms will behave. Most genetic engineering techniques do not allow such specificity.

4. Restriction enzymes are used to cut DNA molecules at specific points.

Genetic Engineering: Promise and Threat (p. 450)

DENNIS CHAMBERLAND

Chamberland's article provides an excellent survey of genetic engineering: its origins, its achievements, its prospects, its dangers. As such, it provides a good introduction to the articles that follow. Some of the topics simply raised by Chamberland here (such as patenting genetically engineered organisms, or genetically screening employees) are treated in greater detail elsewhere in the chapter. Since this article was first published in *Christianity Today*, its perspective is generally religious, but it is neither dogmatic nor sectarian in tone. The reservations expressed about genetic engineering are, in fact, the same reservations as might arise in any ethically-focused discussion of the subject. As Chamberland observes (in para. 52), "The abuse of genetic engineering will come from two familiar directions: (1) ill-defined or nonexistent norms of acceptable social direction and (2) disguised social principles of accomplishing one goal by way of another."

Review Questions

1. James Watson (an American) and Francis Crick (a Briton) were the first to discover the structure of the DNA molecule, the basic building block of all life, and the means by which hereditary information is passed from one generation to another. They first published the results of their studies in 1953. For their achievement—the basis of all subsequent work in genetic engineering—they were awarded the Nobel Prize.

2. *E. coli* is a single cell bacterium. Its biological simplicity (as opposed to the complexity of a human cell) assured that experimenters were able to study the effects of mutating and recombining (splicing) its genetic material.

3. Soon after their formation, genetic engineering companies were able to produce—for a fraction of their former cost—*interferon,* a cancer-fighting agent; *human growth hormone,* to correct pituitary deficiencies; and *human insulin,* to treat diabetes. Scientists envisage using recombinant DNA technology to treat thousands of other genetic disorders. In addition to such medical applications, genetic engineering can be (or will be) used to improve agricultural yields, to fight oil spills, to retard aging, and even to reconstruct species on the verge of extinction.

4. Possible abuses of genetic engineering: creating new agents of biological warfare, using genetic screening as part of the employment application process, engineering "perfect" human beings (somewhat like the Central London Hatchery in *Brave New World*), cloning human beings.

5. Chamberland sees the threat in genetic engineering less in the technology itself than in the principles by which it is applied. Just as nuclear technology can be used to improve life or to destroy it, genetic engineering holds both promise and threat. Chamberland acknowledges the complexity of the moral issues involved, argues against simplistic solutions "that try to capture vague fears," and maintains that Christians (among others) should try to exert influence by emphasizing values, as well as technology.

Perfect People (p. 460)

AMY VIRSHUP

This article raises disturbing ethical dilemmas. The underlying question is a central one in our technological age: now that we have this new capability, this new knowledge, what do we do with it? More specifically, now that we are able to detect genetic defects before birth, what—if anything—do we do when we discover them? The parents interviewed by Virshup give different answers. As is the case with other highly charged issues, such as abortion, capital punishment, or vivisection, students will tend to sympathize with one position or other according to their pre-existing ethical or religious beliefs, rather than the logic (to the extent there is logic) behind the positions. But, as Virshup points out, the issue is not simply whether one side or the other is right, but also the kind of ideal standard of perfection that lies behind the genetic testing of fetuses. How, exactly, do we define a defect? At what point does the identified defect become so great that abortion is an acceptable alternative? What degree of mental retardation? What degree of deformity? Is the world of genetic testing that Virshup describes a "brave new world"—in Huxley's sense?

Review Questions

1. A tentative pregnancy is one that will be carried to term only when the results of lab tests reveal that the fetus has no serious genetic defects. The term became the title of a book on the subject by Barbara Katz Rothman.
2. Though Gilbert's test appears about 95 percent accurate, cystic fibrosis specialists and the CF Foundation have kept their distance, primarily because the test is too closely associated with abortion.
3. Kingsley considers herself a feminist, and as such, might be expected to take a pro-choice position on abortion. (Most pro-choice advocates believe that a woman has an absolute right to control her own body, including abortion, if she deems it necessary.) Just as Kingsley believes in equal rights for women and minorities, however, she also believes in the rights of the handicapped, born and unborn. So, on this issue she finds herself allied to right-to-lifers and others on the political right.
4. Genetic testing is going to become ever more widely available in the next few years, and statistics reveal that a considerable percentage of those who take the tests abort fetuses found to be defective. Many also feel that over time, the reasons for which fetuses are aborted will become evermore frivolous (for example, parents not wanting a fetus with a relatively mild defect or a fetus of a certain sex).

The Total Gene Screen (p. 472)

MORTON HUNT

Hunt's article deals with another problem created by the new technology of genetic engineering: should employers be permitted to screen prospective employees for genetic problems that may render them unsuitable for employment? Proponents argue that such testing helps ensure safe working conditions; opponents maintain that it invades privacy. Like Virshup, Hunt does not take sides in the controversy; rather, he systematically describes the situation and allows readers to draw their own conclusions. The article begins strongly with a case study; surveys the kinds of genetic problems that can be dangerous in certain work environments; outlines some of the history of "hypersusceptibility" research, including the objections that were raised to such research in the 1980's; discusses five "moral dilemmas" created by genetic screening; and concludes with a general prediction about the legal resolution of such dilemmas.

Review Questions

1. Geneticists claim that many diseases are caused by an altered or misplaced gene in a DNA molecule. The minority of people who have these

variant genes are far more susceptible to disease than those who do not. Accordingly (according to genetic theory), cures for such diseases depend upon replacing the defective genes with normal ones, in the hopes that the reconfigured DNA molecules will replicate in sufficient numbers to cure the disease.

2. Genetic screening is frequently seen as a violation of civil rights, particularly the rights of privacy, equality, and freedom of choice. Moreover, since a number of diseases primarily afflict certain nationalities or races, testing for such diseases can be viewed as racist—as a means of weeding out certain "undesirable" groups from the workplace.

3. Many companies consider that it is in their interest to conduct genetic testing to avoid high payments of workers' compensation and damage suit awards and to reduce their employees' health and life insurance premiums. Companies are also concerned with not violating OSHA (Occupational Health and Safety Act) regulations governing worker safety.

4. Hunt predicts that, as in the past with genetic engineering, the opponents will at first gain the upper hand and levy various restrictions; eventually, however, he believes that representatives of the two sides will compromise, to the benefit of all.

A Heretic's View on the New Bioethics (p. 482)

JEREMY RIFKIN

This selection is a combination of two separate sources: a portion of Rifkin's book, *Algeny,* and an interview with Rifkin by a *Science Digest* writer. To many scientists, Rifkin must seem like a crazy man—someone who, in effect, wanders wild-eyed through the streets carrying a sign warning of the world's approaching end. Actually, as these selections show, Rifkin is quite articulate and rational. The gap between the myth and the man is amusingly crystallized in the first sentence of "Jeremy Rifkin Just Says No," a *New York Times Magazine* article by Edward Tivnan (16 Oct. 1988): "Giant Killer Tomatoes . . ." With a frustrated shake of his head, Jeremy Rifkin says the three words most likely to find a place in his obituary; then he laughs and proceeds to polish off a dish of apple pie and ice cream."

Actually, Rifkin's objections to genetic engineering may sound a familiar note to anyone who has studied the attacks on science and technology from the time (perhaps around the time of Copernicus and Galileo) when they began to threaten the established order—or the way that people viewed the established order. This is not to argue that Rifkin is merely a hidebound conservative, afraid of innovation because it threatens his own worldview. Indeed, the kinds of general reservations he expresses (as opposed to the specific analogies he draws between genetic engineering and the Nazis' eugenics programs) are not unlike the reservations expressed by satirists like Huxley in *Brave New World* (or, for that matter, by some of the people interviewed by Amy Virshup). Rifkin sees a brave new world, indeed, and he doesn't like it. Such skepticism is deeply permeated into our arts and popular culture. In the 19th century it was expressed by (among others) Mary Shelley (in *Frankenstein*) Whitman ("The Learned Astronomer") and Hawthorne ("The Birthmark"). And the theme of more than a few science-fiction films of the 1950s was that science was interfering with the natural order of things or creating more problems than it solved ("Them," "The Beast from 20,000 Fathoms," "The Day the Earth Stood Still"). Still, it is one thing to sincerely express skepticism; it is another to become a "Luddite" (as Rifkin's critics have charged) and to try to smash the machinery—or in Rifkin's case, to try to legally block certain types of genetic experimentation. Rifkin would probably be considerably less controversial had he confined his objections to his writings and his speeches and not taken up an activist role. Nonetheless, it may be possible to dispassionately study his ideas, as expressed in the two passages that make up this selection, and to draw some conclusions about both the validity and the value of his ideas on genetic engineering—and how genetic engineering exemplifies the problems with modern science and technology.

Review Questions

1. By "desacralization" of life or of nature, Rifkin means that modern scientists, and particularly bio-engineers, no longer consider living organisms as discrete structural or biological entities (dog, human, etc.), but rather as patterns of information—represented by their distinctive genetic codes—that can be manipulated at will by genetic engineers. According to Rifkin, Darwin began this process of desacralization by postulating Nature as "an aggregate of standardized, interchangeable parts assembled into various functional combinations."

2. Eugenics is concerned (in its negative form) with the elimination of unfavorable physical and mental characteristics and (in its positive form) with the preservation or reinforcement of favorable characteristics. In the 1920s certain U.S. immigration laws were designed with eugenic purposes in mind. Far more catastrophic was the infamous Nazi eugenics program which resulted not only in the selective breeding of superior Aryan specimens, but also in the extermination of millions of "inferior" people. Since genetic engineering involves the manipulation of genetic strings in organisms in order to eliminate undesirable characteristics and to create or reinforce favorable characteristics, it carries about it an aura of eugenics. But while the old eugenics was grounded in social doctrine and ideology, the new eugenics is grounded in economic and utilitarian considerations.

3. Rifkin is opposed to the kind of scientific application—technology—that

seeks to change or control nature through the use of "inordinate power." He believes, for instance, of nuclear power, as of genetic engineering, that the "inherent power of the technology was so inordinate that its mere use—regardless of the intentions of those using it—was irresponsible." Rifkin is not opposed to scientific research that seeks an empathetic understanding of the environment.

On the Origin of Specious Critics (p. 495)

STEPHEN JAY GOULD

Gould's withering attack on Rifkin may at first strike students as a somewhat arcane disagreement between two scientists on such musty matters as Darwinian theory. They should be reminded, first, that Rifkin is not a scientist—though Gould does not attack him so much for his lack of scientific credentials as for what he considers Rifkin's "shoddy" and "anti-intellectual arguments masquerading as scholarship." Second, they should understand that the significance of the debate is broader than a simple disagreement between two individuals on the interpretation of particular texts. The disagreement is symptomatic of the dichotomy between those who are suspicious about science and technology, considering them as fundamentally antihumanistic enterprises (frequently placed in the service of an oppressive state), and those who defend these endeavors as promising humankind a healthier and happier future. Gould also attacks Rifkin for what he perceives as his misunderstanding of science and scientific procedure, as well as for his faulty argumentation. However, it is just as unlikely that Rifkin would be converted by Gould's arguments, as that Gould would be persuaded by Rifkin's. Students may enjoy deciding who comes off better in the debate—and explaining why.

Review Questions

1. Gould offers his overall critical reaction to *Algeny* in paragraph 4 of his article.
2. Gould maintains that in *Algeny* Rifkin: (1) misunderstands Darwin's theories; (2) misunderstands the norms and procedures of science; (3) does not respect the procedures of fair argument; (4) ignores several basic procedures of scholarship; and (5) commits many factual errors.
3. Gould agrees with Rifkin's argument that the integrity of the species should be respected; but he rejects Rifkin's contention that most other biological scientists feel otherwise, and he also rejects Rifkin's contention that we should halt experiments and applications in genetic engineering because one day someone may abuse the technology.

What Price Mighty Mouse? (p. 505)

THE EDITORS OF *THE NEW REPUBLIC*

This article, like Virshup's and Hunt's, focuses on another controversial aspect of genetic engineering—in this case, the ethical aspects of patenting new animals. Note that Jeremy Rifkin pops up again here (paragraphs 6 and 15) as a kind of straw man. A few students may be put off by *The New Republic's* somewhat irreverent (some might say smart-ass) prose style; others may find it refreshingly direct. Still others might find the intricate twists of thought difficult to follow. A discussion of audience may be helpful, here. It would account for why this editorial is so different in style from, say, Chamberland's, which first appeared in *Christianity Today,* and which seems almost solemn in comparison. By the same token, both of these articles seem addressed to a different audience from that of Gould's piece, which first appeared in *Discover,* read primarily by people interested in science.

Review Questions

1. According to the writers, genetically engineered organisms may either be manufacturers or products. If they are manufacturers, they make other products (such as insulin or growth hormone); if they are products they may be used directly (for instance, to protect plants from frost). Until recently, scientists were able to engineer only unicellular organisms, such as viruses or bacteria. Now, however, with bioengineers able to design new strains of mice, or even cows, there is considerable controversy over whether such new animals should be patentable, or, indeed, even created.

2. The writers suggest that regulation be accomplished by existing federal structures; for instance, an agency could be created within the Commerce Department to regulate the patenting of new organisms.

3. Whenever a method is developed to produce goods more efficiently than before, those who produce the goods in the old way will suffer, unless they can adapt. This is unfortunate for them, but it is better for society as a whole. Therefore, the writers argue, the economic argument against bioengineering is based on little more than nostalgia.

4. In discussing patents, the writers note that Thomas Jefferson, who helped draft the nation's earliest patent law, the basis of existing law, stipulated that inventors be given a temporary (seventeen-year) monopoly over the manufacture of their invention, in exchange for making all relevant information public. In this way, both the inventors' and the public's interests would be served. The writers of the article believe that this was a wise law and should apply to bioengineered organisms, as well as to inorganic inventions.

On Cloning a Human Being (p. 511)

LEWIS THOMAS

This delightful piece should provide an antidote to some of the heavy moral issues raised by the dilemmas treated in the previous articles. Thomas's prose is a model of clarity and grace—and of deadpan humor, rare in science writers. The author's medical background helps lend authority to his fundamentally serious ideas; and his discussion of what an "effective" clone job would involve should be soberingly instructive to those of us who wish that one thing could be changed, without giving a thought to all the other things that would necessarily have to be changed along with it. Thomas's conclusion is faintly reminiscent of the ending of H.G. Wells's story, "The Man Who Could Work Miracles": wishing merely to extend the daylight a few hours, the newly-omnipotent hero inadvertently stops the earth from rotating, sending everything not attached to the ground—including himself—flying off into space.

BUSINESS ETHICS

11

Aside from being an occasion for student writing, this chapter seeks to introduce freshman to the subject of ethics and to business ethics in particular; to offer models for making ethical decisions; to provide cases upon which students can test those models; and to raise difficult, debatable questions about values in business life and the extent to which these differ from values in personal and family life. The reading selections in the chapter were chosen to match these pedagogical aims. Richard DeGeorge, Gerald Cavanaugh, and Sissela Bok introduce students to the subject of ethics and business ethics. Cavanaugh and Bok provide methods of analysis for puzzling through difficult ethical decisions, models that can then be applied to several cases in the chapter, including a scene from Sinclair Lewis's *Babbitt*. Students will likely debate points throughout the chapter, especially when discussing the cases. The possibilities of debate will be heightened when students read Carr's "Is Business Bluffing Ethical?" Here, Carr maintains that a separate code of ethics applies to business, a code that is dirtier than the one governing personal relations. Students will want to read the critique of his argument quoted in Discussion and Writing Suggestion #6, following the article itself. Students should be urged to compare their own reactions to Carr with those of the many readers of the *Harvard Business Review* who responded to Carr by writing letters to the editor.

Soon enough, many students will find themselves in the working world, and it is all but inevitable that at some point they'll encounter situations where they are asked (or are required) to behave one way when conscience dictates that they behave another. Many students, working their way through school, have already encountered such predicaments, and for these young men and women the cases and models for analysis offered here will be pertinent, indeed. The largest goal of the unit is to inform students that strategies exist for making difficult ethical decisions. Students need not rely on instincts alone in ethically troubling circumstances; indeed, they *should* not, according to several writers in this chapter who believe that *analyses* must be brought to bear so that one can explain the reasons for choosing one action over another.

The Case of the Collapsed Mine (p. 521)

RICHARD T. DE GEORGE

In this hypothetical case of a mining accident, with a style of posing questions but providing no answers, Richard T. DeGeorge does an admirable job of surveying the territory of business ethics. Those who read this piece will know something of the variety of issues important to the business ethicist—and to any business person committed to making "right" decisions. No student who reads the case can fail to be impressed with how one who is sensitive to ethical concerns can draw out ambiguities—can see problems where, to the uninitiated, there are few. Students may be overwhelmed by DeGeorge's success at problematizing the case of the collapsed mine; if so, ask them to choose a single one of his categories of questioning and to reflect on that. You might also tell students that in the reading following this one, Gerald Cavanaugh offers a model for answering many of the questions that DeGeorge raises.

Ethics in Business (p. 526)

GERALD F. CAVANAGH

Cavanaugh provides an important overview of business ethics. He justifies the need for corporate ethics, reviews ethical theories (thereby setting the discussion of business ethics in a broader philosophical context), and then offers a model for making ethical decisions in business. This model (in the form of a flow chart) can be used by students in thinking about the several case studies in the chapter. Students may find it difficult to keep the defining strands of the ethical theories separate. Cavanaugh conveniently provides two tables to help students with the definitions. Students should be urged to read and use the tables, not to memorize definitions.

Review Questions

1. "Each manager [must] possess a set of internalized and operative ethical criteria for decision making" because the alternative is an unacceptable level of government intervention to maintain an orderly and well-functioning world of business. Aside from adversely affecting efficiency and productivity, excessive government intervention would foster an atmosphere where "any transaction that was not witnessed and recorded could not be trusted." According to Cavanaugh, maintaining an ethical society is the best way to ensure a free society.

2. The utilitarian theory of ethics, first proposed by economist Adam Smith, defines a moral act as that which benefits the greatest number of people. Conversely, the rights theory places highest value on the individual's personal and property rights. The justice theory of ethics stresses that any act or policy should be democratic and equitable to the interests of all persons, including minorities.

3. Cavanaugh defines overwhelming factors as "data from the situation which may in a given case justify overriding one of the three ethical criteria: utility, rights, or justice." In other words, there will be times when the criteria cannot be easily applied to a situation because of extenuating circumstances. Two examples are offered in the reading: "incapacitating factors" that "coerce" individuals to behave in a manner they ordinarily wouldn't; and "incomplete information" that prevents individuals from making ethical decisions.

4. A third overwhelming factor is the "principle of double effect," which comes into play when an "act has both a good and a bad effect." In deciding whether or not to go forward with the act, a person should pose three questions: First, is the act intended to result in a bad effect? Second, is the bad effect intended as a means to a good end? Third, does the good end sufficiently justify the bad effect?

Whistleblowing (p. 543)

SISSELA BOK

Sissela Bok introduces an important concept in business ethics—whistleblowing—and then provides a series of questions that people in business can apply when in doubt about exposing suspected improprieties among workmates. Like Cavanaugh, Bok offers conceptual tools students can use in responding to the case studies in the chapter. Note that Review Question #4 asks students to organize the questions (according to three criteria) that Bok believes can help one decide whether to blow or "swallow" the whistle.

Review Questions

1. A whistleblower is an individual who reveals "negligence, abuses or dangers that threaten the public interest." The revelation is based on "inside" or specialized knowledge, and the whistleblower is frequently associated with the very organization against which the accusation is made.

2. The "insider" who contemplates blowing the whistle must confront issues of "loyalty, conscience, truthfulness, [and] personal and career concerns."

Outside pressures may be brought to bear when, for example, there is a conflict between the (potential) whistleblower's duty to one's clients and colleagues and the code of ethics that elevates one's responsibility to the public above private interests. Additionally, the likelihood of retaliation is a key factor the whistleblower must consider. Sanctions may be brought against the whistleblower both by a public that would rather not acknowledge the problem as well by those who are the subject of the allegations.

3. If the whistleblower's warning turns out to be inaccurate, untold and irreversible harm may be done to innocent individuals. Alternately, if a minor situation is brought to public attention when it should either have been handled through private channels or have never reached the public at all (e.g., in denunciations of a worker's sexual preferences), the accused might unfairly be denied an opportunity to vindicate him- or herself before a public that has been improperly biased.

4. *Dissent*
   a. Is the outrage so blatant or the danger so great as to warrant whistleblowing?
   b. Is whistleblowing premature? Is evidence insufficient? can alternate, inside channels be explored?

   Breach of Loyalty
   a. Are there inside remedies that could both resolve the problem and maintain the dual loyalty to private and public interests?
   b. Is there sufficient time to explore inside remedies before blowing the whistle— or are the dangers to the public imminent?

   Accusation
   a. Is the method chosen to remedy the situation (inside versus outside) too extreme and likely to deny the accused a "fair hearing"?
   b. Is the issue to be exposed really in the public interest?
   c. Has the whistleblower accepted responsibility for blowing the whistle—that is, made him- or herself known, as opposed to remaining an anonymous tipster against whom the accused cannot mount a defense?

Cases for Analysis and Discussion (p. 553)

The three cases for analysis and discussion offer students an opportunity to analyze and take a stand on one hypothetical and two actual situations in which individuals are compelled to act in ways that compromise them ethically. You might point out to students that these cases lend themselves to rich and complex investigations, provided students are alert to ethical concerns. (Recall how DeGeorge was able to draw out dozens of questions from the case of the collapsed mine.) Students should remain open to ambiguity, here. They should base responses to the cases on *explicit* criteria, or guiding questions, such as the ones offered by Cavanagh and Bok.

Is Business Bluffing Ethical? and Showdown on "Business Bluffing" (pp. 574, 588)

ALBERT CARR, TIMOTHY B. BLODGETT

Albert Carr's article in the *Harvard Business Review* (HBR) caused an immediate firestorm of reaction, and it is for this reason we include here along with the article a sampling of that reaction. Carr's thesis is that different standards of morality apply to the world of commerce than do to one's private world of family and social relations. Student reaction may well divide along the lines reported on by HBR editor Timothy Blodgett, and the differences of opinion should provide a fine occasion for debate. Following Carr, Blodgett edits letters of response from HBR readers, some of whom vigorously denounce Carr's philosophy as cynical, others of whom accept Carr's thesis grudgingly and wish the world were otherwise. As with the three cases for discussion, the issues here are highly charged, and students should be encouraged to respond with an *analysis* based either on the models offered by Cavanaugh and Bok or on other criteria that students clearly define. (Note: In Discussion and Writing Suggestion #6, students will find a critique of the key assumption in Carr's argument.)

Review Question

1. Unlike other authors, Carr makes a distinction between standards of business ethics and standards of personal or religious ethics. Carr describes a situation in which personal or religious ethics has no place in business, which is governed by a "game ethics" similar to that of poker. If businessmen or women want to survive in the world of business, they had better become adept at the "game."
2. In comparing business ethics to the ethics of poker, Carr notes several similarities, such as the "element of chance," the importance of "steady skill," and knowledge of both the rules and the opponent's strengths and weaknesses. He goes on to assert that no one expects the poker player to be motivated by personal or religious morals. The skillful player is expected to bluff and, most importantly, to win. In poker, the unfair player is the one who, "while abiding by the letter of the rules, finds ways to put other players at an unfair disadvantage." Unlike personal ethics, the ethics of poker calls for distrust, ignores friendships, and encourages deception.
3. According to Carr, decisions in business are governed by strategy, not ethics. The two are sometimes confused because "non-players" assume that business ethics are synonymous with personal ethics. The confusion is compounded when a "player" does act in a moral way. The public assumes the player acted out of ethical responsibility when in fact he or she was simply using a business strategy.

4. In addition to the psychological strain that results when personal ethics collide with business ethics, the individual may suffer criticism from "non-players" such as family members or friends who are unaware of the distinctions between personal and business ethics. Conversely, the player who chooses the "moral route' risks being labeled by associates as an "oddball or radical."

Babbitt (p. 597)

SINCLAIR LEWIS

Sinclair Lewis's story of George Babbitt appears as the final "case" in this chapter—but, being literature, it is more. Because of Lewis's talents, readers gain access to the motivations of characters in ways not possible in the other cases. Motivations here are complex: actions follow from motivations, and descriptions of actors are piquant and memorable. As with the other cases, student reactions can be expected to split—in this instance on the question of whether or not Babbitt has done anything wrong by "buying low and selling high." Students will likely debate differences between what is "legal" and what is "right." As with their responses to other cases in the chapter, students should be encouraged to be analytical here. If Babbitt is justified in conducting the real estate transaction as he does, *why* is he justified? If he is wrong, students should be able to offer their reasons—once again drawing on Cavanaugh's and Bok's models to do so.

AIDS: PUBLIC GOOD VS. PRIVATE RIGHTS

12

AIDS is a subject of more than academic interest to most students. This dread disease has not entirely stopped the sexual revolution in its tracks, but worried teenagers are now considerably more cautious than they were a decade ago. Parents of today's adolescents (who grew up in the liberated 1960s) are often of two minds concerning the AIDS threat and their kids: as parents, relieved that sexual promiscuity is declining; as former teenagers, sorry for their kids who have to be so careful, even fearful about sexual encounters.

The central question of this unit is posed in the title—AIDS: public good vs. private rights. The public has a right to be protected against such deadly threats as exposure to AIDS. This necessarily entails certain restrictions against persons with AIDS and persons carrying the AIDS virus. On the other hand, such persons also have rights—the right to privacy and the right to be protected against discrimination, to name two. To what extent do these rights conflict? When they do conflict, whose rights take precedence? How do we resolve the conflicts?

The key selection—and indeed, the one that inspired the unit—is the one dealing with California Proposition 102, on reporting exposure to the AIDS virus. In a relatively short space, the opposing arguments comprising this selection crystallize the debate over public good vs. private rights, as they apply to AIDS. The form of the selection—part of an informational pamphlet mailed to citizens to help them make up their minds on candidates and propositions on which they will be voting—emphasizes the very real issues of public policy under debate. To provide some context, this selection is preceded by an informational pamphlet from a medical laboratory describing what we know about AIDS, as of the late 1980s. The selections in the middle part of the unit take various positions in the debate—Restak and Buckley arguing for the rights of the public; Nelson and Altman arguing for the rights of the individual. In the final part of the unit, John Tierney shows that the risk of AIDS for heterosexuals is less than had previously been supposed. And in her moving short story, "The Way We Live Now," Susan Sontag portrays the devastating impact of AIDS on the loved ones of the victims.

AIDS: The New Epidemic (p. 616)

ABBOTT LABORATORIES

Of the several pamphlets aimed at educating the public to the nature of the AIDS threat, this one seemed to us the best—concise, logically organized, highly informative. In fact, we believe it serves as a model of how to clearly and objectively present information on a complex, emotionally fraught subject to an understandably worried audience. As such, it could be imitated by students in dealing with other subjects (this is the point of Discussion and Writing Suggestion #3). An exercise like this would compel students to consider the main questions their audience might have about the subject, to determine a logical order for such questions, to adopt an appropriate tone (objective, though concerned, and not claiming omniscience) for the responses, and to marshal the appropriate facts for the responses without getting bogged down in unnecessary detail (i.e., detail that may be appropriate in a medical article, but not in an informational pamphlet). Finally, this selection demonstrates the effectiveness of the question-and-answer format, one that, with modifications, may be adapted for a variety of academic and professional purposes.

Review Questions

1. False. Five to 20 percent of those infected with the HTLV-III virus will eventually develop AIDS or AIDS-related conditions.
2. The AIDS virus is transmitted from one person to another through the exchange of bodily fluids, particularly semen. Such exchange can occur through sexual contact, through the sharing of contaminated hypodermic needles, or upon receiving contaminated blood transfusions.
3. Those at highest risk for AIDS include male homosexuals, bisexuals, intravenous drug abusers, and hemophiliacs.
4. Since there is currently no cure for AIDS (a cure would involve destroying the AIDS virus and revitalizing the body's damaged immune system), treatment focuses on the secondary illnesses cause by AIDS, such as pneumonia and Karposi's sarcoma.

Proposition 102: Reporting Exposure to AIDS Virus (p. 622)

As we noted earlier, this is the selection that inspired the unit. When citizen Behrens received his "California Voter Pamphlet" in the mail, a month or so before the November 1988 election, it struck him how the arguments on each ballot initiative were arranged in the form of a structured debate. After a neutral description by the Attorney General and by the "legislative analyst," one side presents its case in favor of the measure, and the other side offers its rebuttal. Then this second side presents its case against the measure, and the first side presents *its* rebuttal. A perfect way to have students study argument and counter-argument and to weigh their respective merits! Of course, students should be reminded that we live in the real world, where, too often, arguments are won less on the basis of superior logic and evidence than on the basis of appeals to emotion and self-interest. Still, these arguments and rebuttals should impress students with the necessity for anticipating counter-arguments and, therefore, with the necessity for preparing *counter* counter-arguments.

Review Questions

1. Proposition 102 (1) requires doctors and other health care professionals to report the names of persons who test positive for the AIDS virus to public health authorities; (2) restricts confidential testing for AIDS: (3) requires public health authorities to notify the spouse or other sexual partners of a person testing positive for AIDS; (4) removes prohibition on using such tests to deny employment and insurability; (5) makes it a crime for an infected person or one testing positive to donate blood; (6) modifies the fines for unauthorized disclosure of AIDS test results.
2. Several examples: Current law (in California) specifies that AIDS test results must to be kept confidential; the proposed law would require the reporting of positive results to public health authorities. Current law requires that persons cannot be tested for AIDS without their written consent; the proposed law lifts this restriction and allows the involuntary testing of persons charged with certain crimes. Current law makes it a crime for physicians and nurses to report positive test results without written consent of the person tested; the proposed law lifts this restriction in certain circumstances. Current law prohibits using results of AIDS testing as a basis for denying employment or insurability; the proposed law would permit such use of test results.
3. The legislative analyst could not determine exactly how much money Proposition 102 would cost the state of California, since the amount depended upon such unknowable factors as how much it would cost to investigate cases of AIDS and to take all necessary measures to prevent its transmission, and how much it would cost to insure or provide public welfare for persons denied insurance or employment because of positive AIDS tests. The analyst believed, however, that the costs *could* run from the tens to the hundreds of millions of dollars annually.
4. By "THE SYSTEM WORKS," advocates of Proposition 102 mean that the system of required reporting of such communicable diseases as syphilis

works in helping prevent the spread of these diseases. Therefore, they argue, the system should be expanded to include AIDS.

5. Not everyone who tests positive for the AIDS antibody will get AIDS or an AIDS-related disease. Moreover, AIDS testing is not 100% reliable.

When a Plague Looms, Society Must Discriminate (p. 635)

RICHARD RESTAK

Restak favors "the common good" over the rights of AIDS victims. Aware that this position might open him to charges of callousness, he take care at the outset to argue that AIDS victims should be treated compassionately and to insist that *his* position is the truly "humanitarian" one. Restak's central argument is that we don't yet know enough about the AIDS virus and how it is transmitted (and we may not know for decades, since the virus may remain latent for that long) to know for certain how safe it is for persons without AIDS to be exposed, in places like schools and health-care facilities, to persons with AIDS. Until we do know, he argues, it is irresponsible (and "sentimental") to argue that the civil rights of AIDS victims outweigh all public health considerations. In fact, "the threat of AIDS demands from us all a discrimination based on our instinct for survival against a peril that, if not controlled, can destroy this society." Among the questions raised by this article: Is Restak being unduly alarmist? Under what circumstances is discrimination justified? Just how far do the civil rights of AIDS victims extend? What about the survival rights of persons without AIDS?

Review Questions

1. At the outset of his essay, Restak establishes a conflict between the rights of the AIDS victim and the "common good." He believes the latter should outweigh the former.
2. In attempting to check the spread of a disease, society has quarantined victims of scarlet fever, smallpox, and typhoid. Restak suggests that society should apply the same reasoning when faced with victims of AIDS.
3. Restak asserts that we do not yet have sufficient information on how AIDS is transmitted. Moreover, since AIDS has a long incubation period— sometimes years—we will not have conclusive answers about this matter until "well into the twenty-first century." That being the case, he argues, it is foolish to pass antidiscrimination laws that could have the effect of facilitating the spread of AIDS.

Blaming the Victim (p. 641)

JAMES B. NELSON

Nelson's article serves as a counterpoint to Restak's. Challenging Restak's assertion that we don't know enough about how AIDS is transmitted, Nelson argues that "Overwhelming data now make it clear that the chances for contracting the [AIDS] virus through nonsexual contact is almost negligible." (It should be pointed out, though, that Nelson—unlike Restak—is *not* a physician.) Thus, Nelson, while not responding directly to Restak, might accuse him of helping to spread "hysteria" over AIDS. Like Restak, Nelson squarely addresses the issue of "individual rights versus the social good," but argues that it has not been demonstrated that the social good depends upon the withdrawal of civil rights of AIDS victims. The heart of Nelson's article is the set of five criteria that he urges we use to help weigh the competing claims of individual rights and social good. Without flatly asserting that the former should take precedence over the latter, the clear thrust of his article is toward this conclusion. Your students may be interested in speculating on the extent to which Nelson's sentiments are particularly "Christian." To what extent might non-Christians share these views, if they were expressed in an entirely secular context?

Review Questions

1. Since most AIDS victims are homosexuals, since the genesis of the AIDS epidemic is associated with Haiti and with African countries, and since most intravenous drug abusers are black, fear of AIDS has been transferred into additional fear and hatred of an already homophobic and racist society, according to Nelson. Nelson further maintains that because AIDS is highly prevalent among gays and blacks, society gives low priority to AIDS in funding adequate treatment and research toward a cure.

2. Many people believe that homosexuality is both a freely chosen lifestyle and an immoral one. Since this freely chosen, immoral lifestyle leads frequently to AIDS, the victims of AIDS (according to the blame-the-victim mentality) have no one to blame but themselves for their condition.

3. According to Nelson, AIDS victims are entitled to adequate health care and to privacy. They have received sufficient quantities of neither, he charges.

4. The Church's traditional condemnation of homosexuality has thrown the weight of religious institutional authority behind homphobia. It has also created a climate of moral intolerance of homosexuals.

The Moral Crusade (p. 648)

DENNIS ALTMAN

In this selection Altman goes beyond the pro-con arguments on restricting the civil rights of AIDS victims to probe the depths of the irrational fury often leveled at persons with AIDS. For Restak, who does favor certain restrictions, this is an entirely medical issue. But for many others, as Altman shows, it is a moral issue, a religious issue. Like the Black Death in the 14th century, considered an instrument of God's justice, AIDS is sometimes seen as divine retribution for immoral sexual proclivities. So AIDS victims become "sex-crazed degenerates," and we find an Australian legislator saying that he "hopes that no one finds a cure for [AIDS]."

Of course, not everyone who favors public over private rights on this issue does so for primarily moral reasons. But this article should demonstrate to students that the debate over the civil rights of AIDS victims (like many other public debates) is not entirely a rational one; and it cannot be won or lost entirely on rational grounds. Rationally, for example, there is no reason to pass a constitutional amendment making flag-burning a crime. But enough people have such deep-seated emotional feelings about the flag and about patriotism that this issue—like the AIDS issue—is not likely to be decided by the triumph of good reasoning over bad.

Review Questions

1. Since the spread of AIDS was linked to a homosexual lifestyle of which the fundamentalists disapproved (and since this lifestyle was set in the larger context of shifting sexual mores), they were quick to establish a moral significance to the epidemic.
2. In addition to writing letters-to-the editor, anti-gay activists have attempted to block or reverse legislation decriminalizing homosexuality, to ban gay groups and events, to challenge anti-discrimination in employment laws, and—in extreme cases—to resort to physical violence.

Identify All the Carriers (p. 653)

WILLIAM F. BUCKLEY, JR.

Buckley's short article is probably the most provocative in the chapter, and students should enjoy being outraged—once they overcome the language barrier (if this is their first encounter with Buckleyese). Actually, in the first part of his article, Buckley presents a reasonable summary of the opposing points of view represented by the "public" and "private" sides of the AIDS debate. It is only when he begins his dialogue between School A and School B (to which he belongs) and then goes on to suggest sterilization and tattooing of AIDS victims that we realize we are entering a new dimension in our coverage of the subject. Ask students how Buckley's "utilitarian" ideas compare to Restak's on this subject. Ask them also what they think of his contrast between his proposed tattoo and the notorious "Scarlet Letter," and of his assertion at the end that "in order to fight AIDS, we need the civil equivalent of universal military training." Above all, ask them to determine exactly what it is that they dislike (if, indeed they do) about the tattoo proposal.

Review Questions

1. Essentially, School A represents those whose primary concern is the hard-won civil liberties of homosexuals. School B's primary concern is the protection of the general public.
2. A paraphrase: Some of the people worried about AIDS, who advocate laws designed to check its spread, claim to be primarily concerned with public health. They probably are, but they also have a private agenda: they would like to revoke the civil rights of the homosexuals that they despise.
3. Buckley believes that soldiers who test positive for AIDS should be "discreetly discharged"; that an AIDS test be required, along with a conventional blood test, for a marriage license, and that those testing positive be sterilized; and that, "in rapid stages," in the course of normal institutional screening (such as for medical insurance), everyone in the population be tested for AIDS.

Straight Talk (p. 658)

JOHN TIERNEY

The main purpose of Tierney's article is to provide re-assurance to those so terrified of the dread "Heterosexual Breakout" in this age of AIDS that having sex has come to seem like playing Russian roulette. Tierney does not provide any guarantees, of course, but he demonstrates with impressive clarity and logic that with reasonable precautions taken, casual heteroesexual activity (and even casual contact with AIDS victims) is considerably less dangerous to the health than smoking cigarettes. Tierney begins with the striking image of the Demon of the Pestilence—a 17th century apparition that appears to have returned in the late 20th century. After briefly surveying the state of panic that AIDS has created, Tierney focuses on "the Kojak of AIDS," Anastasia Lekatsas, a New York City AIDS investigator, whose interviews with AIDS patients convinced her of the miniscule possibility of contracting the disease from hetereosexual activity alone. In the next section, Tierney focuses on the question of "risk analysis," and notes some interesting inconsistencies in the way that Americans view the comparative risks of various activities. For example, no one wants to live near a nuclear power plant, though not one American has ever died in a nuclear power accident; but few give a second thought to driving their vehicles every day, a far more hazardous activity, involving thousands of deaths every year.

This article orginally appeared in *Rolling Stone,* a "hip" magazine; the language crackles with wit and imagination. Alluding to Dr. Helen Singer's remark, Tierney calls the AIDS-driven fear of sex "the Lost Starry Nights Factor." He compares the odds of contracting AIDS in a hetereosexual encounter, when a condom is used, to "dying during the next three months by being hit by an airplane falling out of the sky." And he ends, as he begins, with the frightening image (though somewhat less frightening at the end) of the Demon of the Pestilence.

Review Questions

1. Tierney's main purpose—as he explains in paragraph 7—is to explore the question of whether or not AIDS poses a serious threat to the heterosexual population.
2. The Hispanic AIDS patient had initially been classified by the hospital as NIR—no identified risk, indicating that the man did not fit any of the high-risk categories for AIDS. Extensive questioning by Lekatsas, however, revealed that the man had engaged in homosexual activity. This added one more link to the chain of evidence suggesting that hetereosexuals with no other risk factors (intravenous drug abuse, hemophilia, transfusion, etc.) were highly unlikely to contract AIDS. Lakatsas' conversation with the man casts doubt on the reliability of statistical information about AIDS because it show how AIDS victims, frequently ashamed, will often lie about how they contracted the disease when responding to question-naires—the basis of much statistical information.
3. The hysteria about AIDS is not only unwarranted, Tierney believes, but also dangerous, because it tends to promote homophobia and prejudice toward AIDS victims.
4. Tierney uses an increasingly unlikely series of statistical possibilities—ranging from your risk of being killed in a car accident sometime during your life, to the chance of Chicago being leveled by a giant asteroid—to illustrate the unlikelihood of various kinds of heterosexual encounters resulting in AIDS.

The Way We Live Now (p. 671)

SUSAN SONTAG

Students' first reaction to this story may be to throw up their hands in frustration at the long, run-on sentences. But if they can get past this narrative technique, the story should become perfectly lucid to them, and in most cases, very moving. Perhaps it will help to look closely at the first sentence, as an example, and sort out the various points of view and events described. If we were to break up this sentence into several smaller sentences, so that each new sentence contains no more than one thought or statement attributed to one person, we would generate something like the following:

MAX (to Ellen): At first, he was just losing weight. He felt only a little ill.

GREG: He didn't call for an appointment with his doctor because he was managing to keep working at more or less the same rhythm.

TANYA: But he did stop smoking, which suggests that he was frightened, but also that he wanted, even more than he knew, to be healthy, or healthier.

ORSON: Or maybe just to gain back a few pounds.

TANYA: He told me that he expected to be climbing the walls (isn't that what people say?) and found, to his surprise, that he didn't miss cigarettes at all and reveled in the sensation of his lungs' being ache-free for the first time in years.

Some of these statements may be paraphrases, rather than direct quotations, and part of the statement attributed above to Tanya may actually have been spoken by Orson (the text is ambiguous on this point). But both the exact words and the precise attribution of the words is less important than the distinctive atmosphere conveyed by Sontag's prose. Spelled out as above, the dialogue might be from a soap opera. Artistically transformed by Sontag, these fleeting conversations, completely divorced from their immediate context, and unified only by the developing reality of the dying victim, give an impression of confusion, uncertainty, hope, fear—and love. As art often does, this story works by "making strange" everyday events so that we can look beyond the familiar surfaces and see reality in a new light.

BARTLEBY: WHY DOES HE PREFER NOT TO?

13

We selected "Bartleby" as the subject of our casebook for several reasons. First, we like it: we think it's a fascinating and compelling story. Second, although "Bartleby" is easy enough to comprehend on the surface, its "true" meaning could be almost anything—and so it becomes a puzzle to figure out. Third, since representatives of almost every school of literary criticism have tried their hands at solving this puzzle, students who read through some of this criticism are exposed to a broad spectrum of possible responses. As we've tried to emphasize in our headnotes, however, these varying interpretations are not mutually exclusive. Simply because one leans toward, say, an autobiographical explanation of Bartleby's behavior, one is not thereby prevented from subscribing simultaneously to religious or psychological explanations. Most of the authors of these articles would probably agree that their analyses were not meant to be reductive or one-dimensional.

We have retitled all of the articles, for the sake of emphasizing the contrasting approaches. Thus, Morris Beja's "Bartleby Is a Schizophrenic" offers a psychological explanation. H. Bruce Franklin's "Bartleby Is Christ" focuses on the Christian dimension of the story. Louise K. Barnett's "Bartleby Is Marx's Alienated Worker" provides a Marxist approach. Leo Marx's "Bartleby Is Melville" (retitled from "Melville's Parable of the Walls"), an autobiographical approach, is probably (among Melville critics) the most well known, and widely accepted, of the pieces reprinted here. Finally, Patricia Barber's "Bartleby Is a Woman" suggests what is perhaps the most novel reading of Melville's story.

Bartleby, The Scrivener (p. 693)

HERMAN MELVILLE

Perhaps the best advice to give students encountering "Bartleby" for the first time is to read it uncritically, as if it were just another story. We would not color their responses in advance by emphasizing the fact that most people have found "Bartleby" extremely puzzling or by emphasizing the variety of critical approaches that attempt to solve the puzzle. After they have read it, students may be asked, through the "Discussion and Writing Suggestions," to formulate their preliminary responses—to the narrator, to Bartleby, to the other employees in the office, to the Wall Street setting, to the prison, to the epilogue. And of course, they can venture to say what it all means. Only after this point will they be mentally prepared to undertake the critical essays that follow.

Melville's story will not appeal to everyone. One problem students may have is that it is not (obviously) a modern story, and so the language is a bit archaic. And since "Bartleby" is not long on action, it may strike some students as slow moving. On the other hand, the story has humorous elements that are (surprisingly) unacknowledged by any of the commentators that follow. Most obviously, there's a sense of the ridiculous about the basic situation and its various offshoots that, at least to some extent, is quite comical. Then there are Melville's humorous descriptions of the other members of the office staff—Turkey, Nippers, Ginger Nut—and their interactions. There is ironic humor at the expense of the narrator and his sense of dignity—in particular, his discomfiture at being made to wait outside his own office and his later confusion about how to explain the situation to his colleagues, who have trouble understanding an employee who refuses to do any work, but who is nonetheless kept on. This is not to say that there are enough laughs in Bartleby to turn it into a TV sitcom. Still, the elements of humor and irony do help to relieve what might otherwise by a fairly grim story.

Bartleby Is a Schizophrenic (p. 725)

MORRIS BEJA

Like most articles focusing on abnormal psychology, this one is somewhat dense—but not overly so, we think. Having already read "Bartleby," (and been sufficiently baffled by it), students should be receptive to (if not grateful for) any explanations of the protagonist's behavior; and there's enough "psychobabble" pervading modern culture so that a psychological analysis should be reasonably familiar, and even plausible. Not that we consider Beja's analysis psychobabble: the actual case studies he cites (and the insights from R. D. Laing to which he frequently refers) resemble Bartleby's case closely enough so that his making the connection seems quite reasonable. The question is, does such an explanation limit the significance of Melville's story? Beja would be the last to answer this question affirmatively. As he emphasizes in his first paragraph, "The mistake is to take an either/or approach: either "Bartleby" is a psychological study, or it is a socioeconomic one, or a metaphysical one, or an existential one, or an autobiographical one, and so on." In other words, the psychological explanation can comfortably co-exist with other interpretations.

Bartleby Is Christ (p. 739)

H. BRUCE FRANKLIN

In this secular age, Franklin's religious interpretation may make less sense to students than Beja's psychological one. But Franklin makes his case well, and he may sway a number of readers to his viewpoint. Actually, we believe that Franklin's essay is literary criticism at its best: through insight and imagination—as well as a close reading of the text—he illuminates the work under discussion, imbuing it with unexpected meaning, significance, and even beauty. We may not, finally, agree with Franklin, but he forces us to consider the story of Bartleby anew, to come to grips with it, as we attempt to integrate his analysis with our prior knowledge and understanding of the story. In any case, it is a powerful (and, we think, plausible) enough interpretation so that our experience of "Bartleby" will never quite be the same again.

What if students make the familiar objection: But did Melville really intend us to come away with this (or that) explanation? How do we *know* he meant such and such? The familiar answer (c.f., the intentional fallacy) remains the same. In the final analysis, it doesn't matter what Melville meant or intended. Even if he didn't consciously intend a Christian interpretation (for example), he and his story may have been indirectly influenced by the Christian mythology (or some other aspect of his culture or upbringing) so that this element found its way into his fiction. But even if he intended no such interpretation either consciously *or* unconsciously, the story is no longer his, but ours; and we are entitled to imbue it with whatever meaning or significance we choose. Of course, such reader-generated meaning may be critically worthless; but if it helps illuminate the work in question for a significant number of readers, then its actual critical value becomes somewhat moot.

Bartleby Is Marx's Alienated Worker (p. 750)

LOUISE K. BARNETT

As a model for government and economic policy, Marxism in the early 1990s is in such headlong retreat, worldwide, that unreconstructed capitalists can almost feel sorry for it. From China to the Soviet Union, from Hungary to

Poland, even in such formerly hardline states as East Germany and Czecho-slovakia, Marx's doctrines are crumbling to pieces, as workers of the Communist world unite in either urging their governments to make drastic reforms—in the direction of market economies—or in simply "voting with their feet" by abandoning their socialist paradises and fleeing to the West. In fact, about the only people these days with a kind word to say about Marxism are the ruling classes of the Communist Party and a few Western intellectuals.

This being the case, is there anything to be said for a Marxist literary interpretation of *anything?*

Actually, we think there's a great deal to be said. As we noted in the introduction, Marxism has always been more effective as an analytical tool than as a blueprint for social reform or for government itself. The ruthless capitalist owner or manager, the oppressed and exploited worker: these are not mythical—or extinct—creatures. Maxism may not be able to provide the answers, but it can certainly ask some very good questions. And it can undoubtably reveal patterns of oppression and exploitation (even when masked under an apparently benign paternalism) in both the real world and in imaginative reconstructions of the real world. So when Barnett looks critically at the apparently benign narrator and asks what kind of a man he really is, and what kind of an office he runs, she is asking some legitimate questions. Does the narrator see everything (and everybody) in terms of his personal property? Is Bartleby a model of the exploited worker? Is his work really alienating? Is his reaction to his alienating work and working conditions a (metaphysically) understandable one? Like Franklin's interpretation, Barnett's which at first may seem off the wall, looks more plausible the more one considers it.

Note that Barnett, like Beja, does not insist that her interpretation is the only possible one. In fact, in her final sentence, she suggests that the "alienated worker can also be the alienated writer"—thus, unintentionally making a good transition to our next selection—Leo Marx's autobiographical interpretation, "Bartleby Is Melville."

Bartleby Is Melville (p. 758)

LEO MARX

Even though this article is the longest in the chapter, its autobiographical focus probably makes it among the most accessible. It is natural to suppose that authors feel impelled to write about themselves, and students' recollections of their own early attempts at fiction will no doubt confirm this.

Not only is the theme of Marx's article accessible, but the style is clear and the presentation thoroughly logical. In the second paragraph of his introduction, Marx offers his thesis: " 'Bartleby' is not only about a writer who refuses to conform to the demands of society, but it is, more relevantly, about a writer who forsakes conventional modes because of an irresistible pre-occupation with the most baffling philosphical questions." And shortly after-wards, at the beginning of the first section (paragraph 4), Marx explains the significance of the "controlling symbols" of "Bartleby": ". . . it may be said that this is a parable of the walls [Marx's original title was "Melville's Parable of the Walls"], the walls which hem in the meditative artist and for that matter every reflective man." In the remainder of the first part of his article, Marx systematically goes through "Bartleby" in an effort to demonstrate the truth of his proposition. In effect, Marx is offering a protocol (a considerably polished protocol, to be sure) of his own reader-response to Melville's story. We read the story through Marx's eyes.

In the second part of the article, Marx draws explicit connections be-tween Bartleby's plight and Melville's own. And at the end of this part, by the time he draws his final conclusion, "What ultimately killed this writer was not the walls, themselves, but the fact that he confused the walls built by men with the wall of human mortality," the terms "the writer" and "he" are purposely ambiguous. In the third part of the article, Marx attempts to show that "Bartleby" is not [as critic F. O. Matthiessen has asserted] "a tragedy of utter negation," but rather a story that contains the seeds of hope and the possibility of salvation—for the narrator and for Melville, if not for Bartleby. He also shows that though Melville identified himself with Bartleby, he was able to critically distance himself from his protagonist and recognize the spiritual, if not physical death that could result from turning away from humanity and toward the walls. Thus "Bartleby" becomes "a compassionate rebuke to the self-absorption of the artist, and so a plea that he devote himself to keeping strong his bonds with the rest of mankind."

Bartleby Is a Woman (p. 778)

PATRICIA BARBER

Our caution in the headnote is worth repeating. Barber is not claiming that Bartleby really *is* a woman. Rather, she asks us to temporarily imagine him a woman—Miss Bartleby—in order to see how the story's meaning changes for us if we make such an imaginative leap. In particular, she contends that we would thereby see that "Bartleby" is "essentially a love story, a story about a man who is confined in an office setting that forbids intimacy and who comes to love a person he cannot save." Melville's story, Barber concludes, is about human loneliness. Barber contends that "Bartleby" is more about the narrator than about the title character. Like Barnett, she focuses upon the particularly oppressive conditions of the office environment and the stifling work that is performed there. Like most of the other critics, she goes through the story systematically, dealing with each section in light of her interpretation.

For some readers—whose basic reaction may be "She's gotta be kidding!"—it is neither possible nor desirable to make such an imaginative leap. Why not (they may argue) imagine David Copperfield or Holden Caulfield as women—or, for that matter, Shylock or Fagin as Catholics? And doesn't changing such a crucial element in the story thereby change the entire nature of the story—making almost *any* interpretation possible? Perhaps. Perhaps not. But Barber's idea seemed to us so intriguing (and compared to some of the other interpretatiaons of Bartleby, not perceptibly further off the beaten track) that we believe it's worth placing before your students and asking their reactions. Like other stimulating pieces of criticism, this one has the virtue of forcing us to think about the story once again and to re-evaluate it anew, very possibly making additional discoveries in the process.